Bob,
Good friends make for a good life.

So What Are The Guys Doing?

Inspiration about Making Changes and Taking Risks for a Happier Life

---

David J. Figura

DIVINE PHOENIX
In coordination with
PEGASUS BOOKS

Divine Phoenix Books
P.O. Box 1001
Skaneateles, NY 13152
www.divinephoenixbooks.com

First Edition: July 2014

Published in North America by Divine Phoenix Books and Pegasus Books. For information, please contact Divine Phoenix Books c/o Laura Ponticello, P.O. Box 1001, Skaneateles, NY, 13152.

Library of Congress Cataloguing-In-Publication Data
David J. Figura
So What Are The Guys Doing? /David J. Figura– 1st ed
p. cm.
Library of Congress Control Number: 2014943234
ISBN – 978-1-941859-00-1

1. FAMILY & RELATIONSHIPS / Friendship. 2. FAMILY & RELATIONSHIPS / Life Stages / Mid-Life. * 3. FAMILY & RELATIONSHIPS / Marriage & Long Term Relationships. 4. FAMILY & RELATIONSHIPS / Life Stages / General. 5. BODY, MIND & SPIRIT / Inspiration & Personal Growth. 6. FAMILY & RELATIONSHIPS / Life Stages / Later Years. 7. FAMILY & RELATIONSHIPS / Love & Romance

10 9 8 7 6 5 4 3 2 1

Comments about *So What Are The Guys Doing?* and requests for additional copies, book club rates and author speaking appearances may be addressed to David J. Figura at *davidjfigura@gmail.com* or Divine Phoenix Books c/o Laura Ponticello, P.O. Box 1001, Skaneateles, NY, 13152, or you can send your comments and requests via e-mail to *laurasbooklist@aol.com.*

Also available as an eBook from Internet retailers and Divine Phoenix Books
Printed in the United States of America

This book is dedicated

to my best friend,

Chris Neiley,

who was there when

I needed him most

ACKNOWLEDGEMENTS

I am eternally grateful to all the men mentioned in the following pages who willingly and openly shared their thoughts and feelings during formal interviews and casual conversations. Their stories and comments not only made this book, but inspired me along the way to be a better husband, a better father, and a better person.

This book described the real life experiences and comments of real people. I have disguised their identities by changing their names, their occupations and in several instances created composite characters. None of those changes, though, affected the truthfulness of what was said.

I would like to thank my publisher, Laura Ponticello, for her faith in me and in this book. She shares my feelings that men, and the women who love them, will benefit from it. Also, I thank Christine Krahling, for her expert copy editing and suggestions.

I am deeply indebted to Hart Seely, a former colleague at The Post-Standard newspaper whose sage advice steered me away from numerous shoals during the writing process and set me on the right path.

Others who read the manuscript provided great feedback included Michelle and Kevin Rivoli, David Connelly, Janis Barth, John Lammers, and my brother, Paul Figura. Also, Mike Lynch, who inspired me to change my career path; and Ed Hickling, whose words of advice came at an opportune time.

I also would like to thank members of my low-stakes poker club, the guys from the Skaneateles Horseshoe International Team, those who played on my co-ed volleyball team and the guys who fished and hunted with me in recent years—including members of the Johnson City Sportsmen's Club. They all reinforced the fact that having good friends makes for a good life.

Finally, there is my wife, Laura, whose smile, endless support and loving ways never cease to amaze me. Laura, more than anyone else, knows what I went through. She supported this project from the start and graciously allowed me to include intimate details about her and our marriage. In addition, her copy editing and numerous suggestions were invaluable.

Frankly, if it was not for her, I would probably be dead in a ditch somewhere.

So What Are The Guys Doing?

CONTENTS

INTRODUCTION

I smile when I think about my 40th birthday. My wife arranged a surprise party that was attended by numerous friends and family members.

I remember the belly dancer, and sitting on a stool and putting on a funny wig that covered my receding hairline as I opened gifts in front of a laughing, cheering crowd. I lost count of how many beers I downed that evening.

I was given all sorts of bawdy, age-related presents, including the book, *Fly Fishing Through the Midlife Crisis* and a white coffee cup that said "Life Begins At 40."

When I hit my late 40s, though, I was bouncing off the walls—unhappy with myself, the way my marriage was shaping up and the direction in which my job was headed.

Despite being a newspaper editor with numerous acquaintances, I felt I had no close friends. There was no one I could ask to go out for a beer, or to go fishing. There was nothing apart from work, more work—and then family.

I was in a mid-life crisis up to my eyeballs and no amount of fly fishing by myself was going to help that.

My 50th birthday was unmemorable. I told my wife, "No party!" Didn't want one. I had dinner with my family and there was a cake. I received a few cards from in-laws. I bought myself an expensive guitar. Deep down, I wondered, *Is this as good as it gets?*

Things could have taken an ugly turn. They didn't.

My wife and I sought marriage counseling, I changed jobs, actively sought out new friends and new experiences—and wrote this book.

I kept it simple. I related what I went through and what other men from various walks of life told me along the way.

I'm no expert. I'm just a guy who loves the outdoors, sports and his beer. I'm also balding, fighting the battle of the gut, taking high blood pressure medication and getting nagged by my wife and daughter to use teeth-whitening strips.

Coming up with a title wasn't easy. The market is flooded with all sorts of self-help books and magazine articles focusing on women and their problems. I just wanted something that men could relate to.

Then the movie, *Eat, Pray, Love*, came out. The 2010 film is based on the true story of author Liz Gilbert, who following a divorce, takes a year-long sabbatical from her job. According to a promotional blurb, she risks "everything to change her life. In her wondrous and exotic travels, she experiences the simple pleasure of nourishment by eating in Italy, the power of prayer in India, and finally and unexpectedly, the inner peace and balance of love in Bali." Actress Julia Roberts played the role of Gilbert in the movie.

Oh, great! Another account of some woman going off and taking some risks, finding herself and getting her groove back. If a middle-aged man did that, it would be looked upon by many as just another mid-life crisis.

My next thought was: *So what are the guys doing?* when women are off getting their lives together. I concluded that there are a lot of men struggling during middle-age. I was among them. I discovered I was putting too much time and emotional energy in some areas, while ignoring others. My life was out of balance.

I observed that many women seem to be handling these years better. They realize what's important for happiness and are more inclined to take action to make those things happen.

During my interviews, I found that I identified with many of the men I spoke to, felt sorry for a few and was truly inspired by others.

It's my hope that men who read this book will realize they're not alone in what they're facing or thinking, and will be motivated to make some much-needed changes in their lives.

Inertia can be a powerful thing. Many men continue to be miserable because they feel trapped, can't see themselves taking a different path and are afraid to take a risk.

Don't be one of those guys.

CHAPTER 1

RESENTFUL AND LONELY

The indispensable first step to getting the things you want out of life is this: decide what you want.
~ Ben Stein, actor, comedian, writer, lawyer

If you don't get lost, there's a chance you may never be found.
~ Author unknown

It was late August 2004, and I was on my front porch with a friend, Fred, puffing on a cigar and sipping from a tall can of Guinness beer.

I told Fred I was down, but I really did not let on how far I had sunk. We were not close enough for me to do that. I was 51.

I did not mention how I really felt about my 24-year marriage, my job, or even myself. Nor did I tell him about an affair I was considering. About the woman who had looked me up on the Internet and was relentlessly emailing and instant-messaging me, wanting to get together.

This was all *before* I started my diary—before I started reading magazine articles and books about middle-aged guys, and the seismic cultural changes they're currently going through, and how depression and suicide rates are rampant during these years—before the emotional marriage counseling sessions with my wife, Laura…

And yes—before I started interviewing middle-aged guys on how they felt on a variety of topics, including loneliness, friendship, money and sex.

No, what I told Fred that evening was just a small part of the big picture. I told him how resentful I was that my wife and her group of friends were doing more and more with each other, leaving me in their wake.

I am talking about annual weekend girlfriend kayaking getaways in the Adirondacks, traveling once a year to different cities along the Eastern Seaboard, weekly winter indoor soccer and spring softball leagues, with drinks and conversation almost always afterward, plus the growing trend among her friends of all-women—50th birthday getaways and celebrations.

Me? I had little or nothing going. I did not have a best friend, just a few casual friends. My 50th birthday had passed with no party. I did not want one. I bought myself an expensive acoustic guitar instead. I had not fished in more than a year. I did not belong to any sports teams. No all-guy getaways.

As president of the high school girls' varsity soccer booster club, I had dedicated a lot of time and effort—even organizing and taking the team to a nearly weeklong soccer camp. There was no time for a family vacation that year.

An entire summer… no, make that nearly three years had just elapsed, and I had set aside little time for myself. It was time to make a change.

There was a local co-ed volleyball league on Thursday nights during the fall and winter, the same night my wife and her friends were playing indoor soccer. Fred said he would play. He recruited his wife, another couple and a female friend of his wife's. I signed the team up.

The six of us, all in our early to mid-50s, were miserable players. But it really did not matter, at least not to me. I wanted an all-guy activity, but I figured this would do. I was getting out during the week. My wife was with her friends, and I was out doing something on my own.

There was one problem. Nobody wanted to go out for a drink, a pizza or even a soda afterward. Nothing. They wanted to play, walk back out to their cars and just go home. Everybody had to get up early, they said.

In their pajamas by 8:15 p.m., I used to say to myself as I drove home. "So much for a night out!"

After more than a year and a half, I grew bitter. We had several new players, but even after dropping a few hints about going out, there were no takers. I even succeeded in getting all our games scheduled early. I kept asking my teammates (who were all empty-nesters) if they wanted to go out. Nothing.

After one game, I just blurted out that it was really starting to bother me. I offered several options: we go out every time, we go out just a few times during a session, or we just get together for a potluck dinner with our spouses at the end of the game over at my house.

While everyone liked the idea of the potluck dinner, most liked the idea of the occasional night out, but not every week.

Fred, however, was silent on the topic. He then joked, "Why don't we send the women home after we play, then all the guys go out and have a few beers and then we can get together at your house afterward and watch *Brokeback Mountain* (a then-popular movie about a pair of gay cowboys)."

I was stunned. The idea that men wanting to get together on a regular basis had some homosexual connotation was not funny. It was sad.

Bottom line: Fred didn't get it. And unfortunately, many middle-aged guys today don't either. It is not about the volleyball.

CHAPTER 2

FINDING MYSELF IN 'THAT PLACE'

At the core of all anger is a need that is not being fulfilled.
~ Marshall B. Rosenberg, psychologist

Resolve to be thyself; and know that he who finds himself, loses his misery.
~ Matthew Arnold, poet, cultural critic

You do not have to look far. The stories are all around. Stories about middle-aged guys who just chuck it—marriage, kids, even in some cases their careers—in decisions looked upon by many as momentary insanity.

You've heard the following. It goes something like:

What the hell was he thinking leaving his wife and kids for that other woman? His wife has a good lawyer and she's going to take him to the cleaners. He's all screwed up. I never liked him anyway. His wife is so nice… and what about the kids?

Many men cannot imagine themselves in that place, making such a decision, such a radical left turn in life. They laugh and elbow their wives when they see something like a car bumper sticker that says: *Marriage is grand; divorce is 100 grand.*

At age 51, I wasn't laughing. I was in that place. I had a good job as a newspaper editor. I had a lovely wife of 24 years and great children—a daughter, 18, and a son, 15.

Nobody knew or suspected what was running through my head. I was not talking about it to anyone. As far as anyone knew, I was happy, content. Hell, I was president of the high school girls' varsity soccer booster club.

The woman living and sleeping with me every night, though, saw the symptoms: the growing frequency of sleepless nights where I left the bed and slept on the couch, unresolved discussions about sex or lack of, the unexpected and prolonged temper tantrums about petty things. Everything was spiraling downward quickly in our marriage and at the time I felt powerless to do anything about it.

I grew up in a small town, in a suburban neighborhood in Upstate New York, one of four children. My childhood was happy, living in a neighborhood with nearly a dozen male friends my age or close to it. My parents were close with a marriage that was strong.

I played soccer, ran track—even won a state championship in the indoor 1,000-yard run. I was in the Honor Society, president of the Key Club, chief justice of the high school's student court.

I went on to Cornell University and continued to run track. Mulling several career options and changing my major four times, I ended up with a degree in Human Development and Family Studies. I went on to graduate school in occupational therapy at USC in Los Angeles, but dropped out after a semester. I decided to write, but could not get a full-time job in the field right away.

Instead, I opted to use my psychology background and got a day job as a rehab counselor in a sheltered workshop for developmentally disabled adults and began freelancing at night for a local newspaper.

Laura, who was then my girlfriend back in New York, came out to live with me. Two years later I asked her to marry me and she accepted. Around that time I landed a full-time job as a reporter at a small newspaper in Los Angeles.

For the next five years we lived childless, enjoying each other's company, the Los Angeles scene and a host of friends we found through work and recreational soccer teams on which we both played.

We moved back to New York in 1986 when I accepted a job as the city editor of a small paper in Auburn, a small Upstate community. I worked my tail off at the newspaper, and our two children came shortly after. The move back east reconnected us with family. Our children grew up knowing and getting love from grandparents, aunts, cousins. It was, and continues to be, a good thing for them.

Meanwhile, I began putting more and more time into work. I became extremely stressed by all the hours I was working. Apart from the family, there was not much time for anything else. At one point I came down with a bleeding ulcer and was nearly hospitalized. My blood pressure was also continually high.

Laura, realizing the constant stress I was under, urged me to get away with my brother-in-law on his annual fishing trip with a group of his friends. I refused, saying I did not have the time and did not need it.

She ignored my pig-headedness and sent in the check for me to go. I went and I was glad I did. It allowed me to decompress, to relax with the guys, and of course, to fish, which I sincerely love to do. It soon became an annual getaway, something I looked forwarded to and religiously marked on our family calendar year after year.

However, two more job moves followed, which meant relocating to two new communities.

We made it through the early child-rearing years with no scars and an intact marriage. My priority, though, continued to be work, work and more work.

As our marriage and the years flew by, my network of friends evaporated. I did not join any service clubs or recreational sports teams (apart from several years of playing in a racquetball league while living in Auburn). We did not go to church for much of that time.

Then I hit 50. Things began to change in our family dynamic and I was not weathering things well. The kids were busy being teenagers. I am sure my behavior puzzled them.

Laura was busy with her career at a local medical equipment manufacturer. She had worked part-time for years during the child-rearing years, often shouldering much of the parenting role with our kids because of my long hours at work. She managed our finances and often made key decisions on purchases and our vacations each year.

With her full-time job came more money into our household. As the kids were getting independent, she was spreading her wings, finally making more time for herself. That translated into spending more time and money on activities with her female friends. She was going one way, and I another.

She was like a flower blossoming. I was wilting, withdrawing. It did not do much for our relationship. Meanwhile, work was becoming more and more of a grind. I was beginning to lose the passion for journalism that had sustained me for years.

Laura kept telling me when I would throw my tantrums or have irrational mood swings: "When you get like this, I don't even want to be around you." She used to abruptly cut me off and walk out of the room. That would rip me apart inside. I looked upon her as my best friend, my only friend. Yet, I was pushing her away by the way I was acting.

Laura sat down with me one day and suggested that maybe I should start taking St. John's Wort, a natural substance that she read somewhere had mood-altering, antidepressant qualities. I refused to even consider it. I was offended.

Nothing was getting resolved and I became more withdrawn, more resentful. At times, I would take out my frustrations on my kids, raising my voice and getting into arguments with them over various topics. There were a number of times when I felt I was right in what I was saying, but was not communicating in such a way that they would listen.

And it seemed more often than not, Laura would take their side in front of them and me—chalking up my behavior and anger to being nothing more than moodiness because I was hungry, or that I was tired and stressed out from work.

It was a bad family dynamic. I interpreted these interactions as lack of respect for me as a father and as a husband. I often walked away mad, resentful, and I blamed Laura for it all.

Then out of the clear blue came an email from a woman I had dated in my distant past. She located me by Googling my name. Being a journalist with my name on a number of stories and on the newspaper's web site, I was not hard to find online.

Things started off casually with us emailing back and forth. She sent me a picture of herself. The frequency of messages picked up to almost daily. She then started instant messaging me during the late evening. Several of the exchanges were titillating, with sexual overtones.

I was flattered and never breathed a word about it to Laura.

She said she was passing through the city where I worked and asked if we could get together for a bite to eat. I mentioned it to Laura and she thought nothing of it.

"Sure, go ahead," she said, not realizing all the online contact that had transpired beforehand.

Nothing happened. We met, rehashed some incidents I had long forgotten. There was no spark. I told her essentially that I felt she should move on with her life.

Nevertheless, the emails and instant messages continued. At times, when I could not sleep at night I would leave our bedroom and go online, and she would be online as well.

"Could we get together again?" she asked. I mentioned I was going soon to a journalism conference. She responded that, coincidentally, she had been planning to visit an old friend in a nearby community that same weekend. Maybe she could get a motel room, she wrote. I did not respond.

I found myself in a crazy-ass, unfamiliar place. Laura, like I said, was clueless. Pretty soon, she would be heading off herself for her annual three-day, all-girls kayaking weekend in the Adirondacks that fall.

Much to my dismay, Laura announced that she would also be traveling down to Annapolis two weeks afterward to join her sister, sister-in-law and three other friends for another four-day, all-girls getaway. She insisted she had told me months before about it. I had no recollection of her telling me that.

"And it's going to be an annual thing from now on," she added.

During Laura's Annapolis trip, the bitterness inside me grew and grew. That weekend I kept ruminating on what our marriage had become, on my loneliness and how I wanted friends, and on how I wanted parity when it came to spending money on me.

I suddenly reached the point where I decided to chuck it. I was going to do something radical with my love life, and it did not involve Laura.

CHAPTER 3

IT'S TIME FOR A CHANGE—BUT WHAT KIND?

> *Middle Age is that perplexing time of life when we hear two voices calling us, one saying, 'Why not?' and the other, 'Why bother?'*
> ~ Sydney J. Harris, journalist

> *It is utterly false and cruelly arbitrary to put all the play and learning into childhood, all the work into middle age, and all the regrets into old age.*
> ~ Margaret Mead, cultural anthropologist and author

Nothing in life is a given. Things can be taken away from you in a moment's notice. We all know that, deep inside.

We middle-aged guys are at the top of our games in many respects. We are at the peak of our careers, of our money-earning capabilities. It is a time when we should be using all the experience and knowledge we have accumulated to maximize our personal and professional lives.

It is also the time when those burning, penetrating questions make the rounds. *Is this all there is in life? Can't I do better than this?*

I am convinced those two questions are probably the genesis of more affairs and broken marriages, more angst, more problems, more *mid-life crises*—than anything.

I go to the image of the middle-aged guy sitting at his desk at work, plucking a harp with one string, making a single sound. He hopes and prays that action will see him through to retirement. With all we know about today's economy, is that the wisest course? Not really. Then why wouldn't that apply to life in general?

Are you miserable or having doubts about yourself, your marriage, the absence of friends, your job and your health?

Think of the *Wizard of Oz* and the Scarecrow, the Tin Man, the Cowardly Lion. They all had doubts, but they recognized the need to take action. They found out that all along they had the tools—the brains, the heart, the courage—to see things through.

So do you. But are you willing to make the needed changes? That's the question.

The Businessman

Sid, 52, is on his second marriage. He remarried a woman nearly 10 years younger. He talked about his second marriage being a *defining, spontaneous decision.*

"It was a time that I didn't expect to have kids again. My wife didn't necessarily feel she wanted to have kids. She assured me she would be okay without kids. And that changed immediately upon 'I do.'"

As a result, Sid said, he had his vasectomy reversed. He told me he pictured middle age as a time when your children are in their older teens, and when they are getting ready to, or are already, in college. A time when you *focus more on yourself.*

"I don't picture myself as being middle-aged. I kind of skipped over it. Middle age for me is going to be when I'm 62 or 63."

Sid is in a traditional marriage. He sees himself as the sole breadwinner and his wife, who works part-time, as being in charge of the household and the kids. His job requires long hours. He feels the pressure of household finances, his second round of college costs and retirement staring him in the face.

"Women don't... (at least my wife doesn't) understand that kind of thing. It's a responsibility that you don't have time to relax. Women seem to think money drops out of the sky somewhere. Kids go to school, then you go on vacation. It just happens. Magically appears."

He said he has told her, "You find a job that knocks down six figures, go for it. I'll stay home and watch the kids. I would really enjoy that... not worrying whether or not the mortgage got paid."

Sid said he and his wife often do not see eye to eye.

"I'm not a real good psychology game player or manipulator. I'm not a negotiator-type person. I just tell her that's it. She tells me I'm not a good communicator because I don't tell her what she wants to hear. I tell her what she needs to hear."

His biggest concern is that his marriage holds together for his kids' sake.

"That they have a solid and as good a home life as possible... I worry about my wife and me having our issues. What if we don't have things worked out? How long can either one of us put up with not being all that happy and so forth?"

We talked about middle age and how life is more than half-over.

"Once in a while, I find myself doing things I didn't think I'd have the chance to do again, or wouldn't have done because I won't have the opportunity to do again. I was away on business in Alaska and took a plane out and went fly fishing. Cost me $700. I never would have spent that money, but I said the hell with it. I'm not going to be here again."

The Architect

I met Cliff at his house one cold, wintry evening. He is 53, married to the same woman for more than 30 years, with two grown sons—one who keeps boomeranging back home for one reason or another.

"We're empty-nesters in a way," he laughed.

We started talking about middle age, and at first, he denied having anything resembling a mid-life crisis. But as we continued to talk, he eventually revealed two huge, defining moments during his middle years.

The first involved the near-death of his son in a car accident. Cliff said he was in his mid-40s at the time. He opened up about it when I asked him about the importance of faith in his life.

"And there are times where that still plays itself, in little snippets and scenes in my mind—like when I'm driving to work and just a thought, like a wave, it comes over me."

He talked about witnessing two miracles. One of the miracles, he said, was when his son survived the crash. "My son was broken. Broken everywhere. He was in and out of intensive care. It was absolutely miraculous that he lived. I thank God every day for that."

And six months later, Cliff said, one of his son's legs swelled to a gargantuan size. A doctor pulled Cliff and his wife aside at the hospital.

"Basically, he came out, very blunt… 'We've done all we can do. We're going to have to take his leg,'" the doctor announced.

The only other option was an experimental medicine, coupled with another experimental technique used primarily on stroke patients. The doctor gave it very little chance to succeed. The two parents insisted he do it. For 24 hours, it was touch and go. Cliff and his wife prayed. They prayed a lot. The leg was saved.

One thing stuck out during those horrible, intense moments in the emergency room and afterward—apart from his conviction about the power of prayer.

"What I felt and experienced from that, was that women (female friends and relatives) were way, way more… they were in the hospital with us. They were supportive. They organized. They got stuff."

He said that men around him were less involved, less supportive. Often, it came down to (particularly at work) a, *How you doing?* followed by a slap on the back, and nothing more.

When he turned 50, Cliff said, something "struck me right between the eyes." He decided to make a radical change in his work life. He was a principal partner at a local architectural firm. He talked about how work as a partner had become all-consuming, that there was a significant amount that was expected of him in regard to time, finances and responsibility.

"An opportunity came along in which I felt I could simplify, recover some balance." He took the job.

The new job was a struggle, but Cliff said it gave him time to reach out into the community, to volunteer for several boards, to spend more time with his wife, with friends. It did not work out. He ended up coming back to the firm, where he was partner, but in a reduced role.

"I like to be involved in the success of a company, but I also want to practice architecture, and not accounting, or being a business manager."

Cliff is confident he made the right career decisions. He said he got the balance he was looking for.

"Work, family, community friendships—God. There you go."

The College Professor

Ivan, 54, talked about his career as an academic and the sacrifices he made along the way.

"I was in college a long time. It was a grind. I was a young professor. That was a grind too. I postponed a lot of things," he shared, noting he and his wife had one child, a daughter.

His daughter has since graduated from college and Ivan and his wife are now enjoying their empty-nester years. In addition to his teaching responsibilities, Ivan added he has been doing outside consulting work to supplement his income.

"I put a lot of that away. It also went toward things like a new septic system for the house, or to fix the roof or to buy a car," he said.

In recent years, though, he has started to indulge himself and his wife more with that extra cash. They have traveled.

He has also starting spending more and more of it on himself. He loves to bike and bought a new, expensive bicycle. Within the past year, he also started taking flying lessons in pursuit of a pilot's license—an endeavor he figures is going to cost him around $8,000 this year, and probably that same amount every year he continues to fly.

Ivan does not own a plane yet, but he does not dismiss that possibility for some time in the future. He has been mulling the idea of flying for years, but "it always seemed to be cost and time prohibitive."

Within the past year, though, things changed. His college mentor died and two close friends were struck with serious health problems.

"Life is short. I think it takes a couple of years to be a proficient pilot," he said. "What was I going to do? Wait until after I retire? Wait until my late-60s? And then what? I probably wouldn't be able to get my medical certification for the license. It seemed like, *What the hell, I'll do it now!*"

For years he lived life with a philosophy of delayed gratification.

"That's not my thing anymore. We were joking about it just last weekend. I'm now into narcissism. I'm doing my best to be a narcissist."

The Lawyer

Tony, who is married, shared a few beers with me at a local bar. With two kids in college and another in middle school, Tony said he and his wife are already adjusting.

"It's slowly coming down to where we started out, just my wife and I. There was a long period of time where everything was geared to the kids. Kids have practices. Kids have games. Now it's going to revert back to, 'What do we want for ourselves?'"

Tony's attitude about work is if he did not work hard, "Where would I be? Where would my family be? So I don't have a choice about working, but I do have a choice about what I do… that's probably why I've had so many jobs over the years."

At 47, he said he has not had a mid-life crisis, but that his wife would probably disagree. He just bought a motorcycle. He owned one when he was younger.

"When we first moved to New York, I had a motorcycle. We sold it to make the mortgage payment on the first house we owned after I got out of law school. She wouldn't force me to sell it. It wasn't her idea. But there was no way we were going to be able to make that first mortgage payment. So I sold it, and I've regretted it ever since."

So just this past summer, he bought one.

"She looks at it and says, 'You're on this danger kick.'"

Tony laughed about her comment and said there are lots of things he would like to do before he retires.

"I want to hike the Appalachian Trail, drive down the Pacific Coast Highway, from Vancouver down to San Diego. I want to see the Black Hills through the Dakotas, take my time and see that part of the country."

He had always wanted to parachute.

"But I've already done that once. Don't want to do that again," he joked.

On the issue of defining moments, Tony recalls the funeral of a lawyer friend that gave him perspective about how he wanted to run his life.

"I sat in the back at the church, and the current firm members all sat in front, and they made a big show of it. Well, they started giving the eulogies. One was given by a firm partner, about when he started in the firm and he'd been working very hard and working weekends and his family had planned this camping weekend months in advance, and he says to (the deceased)… 'I'm having these clients come into the office on this particular case, I know it's not one of your cases. I've worked a lot of weekends. We've planned this for a long time. It's important to my family.'

"And the partner (the deceased) turned to this individual and said, 'I think you have a big decision to make—whether your family is important, or the firm is important.'

"Then the guy relates (to those at the funeral), 'Of course, I cancelled my camping trip and stayed and I've been very successful, and it's all because of him.'"

Tony said he was thinking to himself, *You've totally missed the point. Why are you guys proud of this?*

He concluded, "At my funeral, I hope they tap a *Guinness* and sit around and tell jokes. *Hey, remember when he did this?* I hope they think about all the funny things that happened when I was with them. Oh my God, if they ever say (what they said at that one guy's funeral about me), I hope they open the casket and shoot me."

Afterthoughts

I noticed there are a number of, what I like to call, "alternative universes" out there. Middle-aged men face a wide variety of personal, financial and familial circumstances.

You have men who have been married to one woman for 20-plus years: those who have blown through one, two or more marriages, and those who are out on the computer dating scene.

You have men who have been laid off or who are just scraping to get by and those for whom money is no problem. You have men who have given up on sex in their marriage, and those who are seeing more ass than a toilet seat. There are those with young kids, teenage kids, no kids, and on and on. Are there any similarities? Trends to consider?

Many of the books and magazine articles I read support the idea that there are seismic cultural changes going on in regard to men and women in this generation.

When it comes to middle-aged men, it appears we are connecting less with friends, joining less when it comes to groups and clubs. Our depression and suicide rates are scary. A 2007 *Newsweek* article on male depression noted the highest suicide rate in men, ages 5 to 75, is the age group between 47 and 54.[1]

And women? Among other things, many are openly seeking more balance in their lives, initiating change, putting a priority on connecting and staying connected with their female friends. An *AARP* magazine study showed that after age 45, some 66 percent of the divorces in this country are being initiated by women. [2]

Why? Because women *can.*

Our generation has witnessed an unprecedented number of women in the workforce, with their incomes and lives coming more and more to resemble those of men. Women now comprise more than 46 percent of the workforce. They are more likely to get college degrees than men. [3]

In 1979, women working full-time earned 62 percent of what men did. In 2011, that percentage rose to 82 percent, according to the U.S. Bureau of Labor Statistics.[4]

Four out of 10 households in this country (with children under the age of 16) now have a mother who is the sole or primary breadwinner—a statistic that has quadrupled since 1960, according to the New York Times.[5]

With those jobs come money (disposable income) and more power in relationships.

I was blown away the first time I Googled "girlfriends and getaways." The business world knows what I am saying. I came up with nearly a million hits on hotels, resorts, restaurants, tour ships and wine country getaway specials.

The search revealed a *Girlfriends Getaways* magazine and the emergence of Red Hat Societies. The *I Love New York* tourism campaign (taxpayer supported) has a Women-Only Weekend campaign. I also found a thelmaandlouise.com website for women who want to travel together without their husbands.

Couple that with the fact that, probably for the first time in this country's history, 51 percent of women in the United States are now living without spouses (up from 35 percent in 1950 and 49 percent in 2000).[6]

But enough of statistics and studies. What does this all have to do with this middle-aged guy? I was depressed, lonely… and there was this woman who was emailing me.

CHAPTER 4

I AM A ROCK, AN ISLAND

If you are lonely when you're alone, you are in bad company.
~ Jean-Paul Sartre, writer and philosopher

Life is full of misery, loneliness and suffering—and it's all over much too soon.
~ Woody Allen, comedian, screenwriter, author

How does an extroverted newspaper man in a small community, with scores of acquaintances, get lonely? Easy.

Throughout the last decade, I put much of my emotional and physical energy into work, work and more work. What was left, I gave to my kids and my wife. I just made a decision, somewhere along the way, that there was no time left for me or having any male friends.

My wife was my best friend—a common response given by many married guys I interviewed. However, there was no one else I could go out with for a beer on a moment's notice to discuss a heavy issue. There was no one I could just hang out with, or hit up for a quick favor, no one I could just call and say, "Hey, let's go fishing tomorrow."

Keep in mind, I did not grow up in the community where I now live. I did not have a group of boyhood and high school friends around that I could readily tap into. After college, I moved around, living in four different places around the country. We relocated to Skaneateles, N.Y. while I was in my mid-forties.

And here I was 51, without any close friends, and doing nothing about it.

Then came the fall of 2005. Laura headed off on her three-day kayak weekend with her soccer buddies, followed by a four-day girlfriend getaway with her sister and friends in Annapolis. They were practically back to back.

That Friday night, when she was in Annapolis, I came home from work and ate dinner by myself. I had no plans. No friends to call. No activities for the weekend. Nothing I wanted to read. Nothing I wanted to watch on TV.

My teenage son was busy with his own things that night. So I went out by myself to the local bar. I ordered a beer, watched about 15 minutes of college basketball and ended up chugging my drink. There was nobody there who I knew.

I got this wild idea. I hopped in my truck and decided on a moment's notice to take the long drive to the community where the woman who had been emailing me lived. I figured I would rent a motel room and then contact her.

On the way out, I drove past my house, thinking about all sorts of things. I was bitter about my wife taking off. How could she do this? How much was she spending? How come I spent so little on myself? Why were we arguing so much lately? I had given up hope.

But I could not shake the image in my head of my unsuspecting son back at the house. What was I going to tell him?

I pulled over about a mile down the road and slammed the dashboard with my fist. My eyes quickly filled with tears. I was an absolute wreck. I could not stop thinking about how unhappy I was. How lonely I had become.

The Accountant

Sam, 49, said to some extent, he has been lonely most of his life. He pointed to the fact that he began stuttering heavily when he was in the 6th grade.

"That took its toll, probably 20 years of my life. I was afraid to speak out, to raise my hand, to take charge of something."

But Sam overcame his stuttering and has tried in recent years to break out of that mold. He was a member of a community group for a bit and tried other activities to get out in the limelight.

He said there are people who have lots of friends… "from high school, and they're always doing things, playing softball with 30 different guys all the time.

"I went down the road, where I don't have a lot of friends, have very few friends. My friends are more like acquaintances," he added. "A lot of people would say, I'm all alone, I'm lonely. That's the norm for me."

Instead of connecting with male buddies his age, he has done a lot of things in recent years with his son, including snowmobiling and cycling.

"I like when my son and his friends play video games. I don't play video games, but enjoy watching them."

Sam really values his time alone—particularly when he is working on his finances. He does not like to travel.

"You know, I don't have any ambitions, other than financially. I'd like to meet my financial goals, and if I do, that's all I really want."

He has reached the point in life where "if I want to do something, I do it. If I want to buy something I buy it. I feel pretty good about myself because I haven't denied myself."

He says people occasionally hit him up for favors: *Hey, can I borrow money? Hey, can I borrow your truck? Hey, can you do this for me?*

Sam emphasized, "I tend not to ask other people. I don't need things from other people. You follow me?"

I asked him who he would call if he was stranded at the local airport on a rainy Sunday night, with no family member available. I asked who he would call to do a favor and come pick him up.

"If it had to be a friend, I don't know who I'd call. I'd probably call my neighbor down the street. He's a similar type guy. He's a very busy guy—spends a lot of time by himself. He would come get me. Honestly, that list of people is very small."

The Human Resources Manager

Pete said he does not belong to any clubs or organizations. He has no best friend or groups of friends he hangs with. He emphasized that personal finances weigh heavy on his mind.

"It's a struggle to get by. My wife hasn't been working very much, and money has been tight. When I got married, my plan was to retire as early as possible, hopefully in my late-50s. That's not going to happen. Something miraculous will have to happen."

He talked about his father, who worked as a plant manager. "He was struggling with money, more than we are, because my mother did not work."

Pete, 55, grew up in a large family. His father was not involved in any outside groups or activities, apart from work and family. And like him, "I feel like the family is relying on me to keep (things) going."

Before he got married, Pete had a couple of friends he hung out with during his college days. They were heavy into darts and dart tournaments.

"During the summers, every night we'd get in my pickup truck, grab a case of beer, drink half of it. (And drink some more) and play darts. It's a wonder we survived."

Then the friends moved out of state.

Since getting married, Pete's wife has taken on the *best friend* role.

"She's the only one that I really spend a lot of time with. I don't hang out with anyone else."

He said his wife "feels like she needs a best friend (apart from him)… and tells me 'Why don't I hang out with friends, too?'"

He emphasized that he does think about his family a lot. Once again, the money thing came up. His wife buys all his clothes for him.

"I feel guilty when I go out and buy an extra pair of pants or something. I have five pairs of pants in my closet and don't need any more. I feel guilty going and buying a pair. It's crazy. I haven't bought a shirt for myself in I don't know how long."

His one main hobby/recreational activity is racquetball. But several months ago, he suffered an injury and has not played since. He has put on 25 pounds, and that is worrying him.

"My blood pressure is up, cholesterol is up. Seriously, I'm considering picking up some kind of other physical activity."

Pete likes the informality of racquetball, of just showing up and playing whoever's at the court that day. He does not see the need to be on any kind of team, or to get affiliated with any kind of group.

"I need to find a sport that I can do on my own, but not get bored."

I asked him about retirement.

"When the kids are gone, I can see going on cruises with my wife. Everything I envision involves her."

The Police Officer

David stopped by my newspaper office one evening to talk. While David, 48, said he was intent on seeing his job through to retirement, his wife, on the other hand, continued her education and now has a graduate school degree. With the kids reaching college age, he said she has the friends and disposable income to socialize and travel if she wants.

"With my wife working, the playing field is leveled, because she doesn't need me to survive." He talked about her taking girlfriend getaways to New York City, to Florida.

"I'd say to myself, *how can she just do that?* But she does."

For a while, when she would leave, he would just stay at home by himself, watching sports on TV, listening to music, taking care of the kids. David said he kept a lot of his resentment inside.

"When it came to communicating, that was one of the downfalls in my relationship. To me, the less I said I felt, the better off things would be. It wasn't true. The less I said, the worse it got."

His wife eventually confronted him about the fact that, "I was just hanging around the house all the time."

She said, "You know, it's not my job to make you happy. That's your job. There's nothing I can do for you, nothing I can say to make you happy. You have to go out and do that yourself."

That was a defining moment for David, who up until this point was clinging to the sexual roles of the child-rearing years while he and his wife were entering the empty nest years. His wife was moving past the traditional role, entering a time when she saw marriage as a partnership, with each partner making space and time for themselves. It was new ground for him.

"I sat down and reflected on it. Yeah, she's right. It's my job, my responsibility to go out make a (social) life for myself."

Soon after, David joined a golf league—then another.

"I just started connecting with some guys. It makes a huge difference." It was a big difference in the way he felt about himself, about his wife, his marriage.

"Because when we first started going out together, I only saw her maybe twice a week. We had different things going on in our lives. But there were those things we had together (and that attracted us to each other)." He said that when he got married, he had it in his head that "life for me stopped, and it's all about family and work." Friends got put on the shelf.

After acknowledging the changes in his relationship with his wife, he started thinking from the perspective that he could "have it all… family and friends. He views his relationship now with his wife as "partnership rather than a dictatorship."

"Even as I talk to a lot of younger men nowadays, they think that's their role… but if you look at your generation, that's not the role you're playing."

He is glad he followed his wife's advice, and now he has a solid group of buddies. He is happier and his marriage has taken a turn for the better. He appreciates and looks forward more to time with his wife.

"I (can) go different places with those friends, because my wife has no problem calling her friends up and planning trips to Florida. Now I got my time, she has her time, and there are things we do together. It makes you whole. You know what I mean? It makes you whole."

Afterthoughts

It is sad when your best and only close friend is your wife, and you are having marital problems. Add to that, social loneliness—the glaring lack of friends, the lack of someone to hang with or to bounce things off of in troublesome times—and you have got a real big problem. That is where I found myself.

I discovered, though, through my interviews and reading up on various research and books about men, that I was not alone. At its extreme, the results of loneliness and depression for middle-aged men can be devastating.

American men are four times more likely than women to commit suicide, according to recent studies. Factors include genetics, health issues, upbringing, career choice and middle age.

Middle age is a time when it becomes clear to many that certain decisions have to or should be made and that those decisions will have an impact in the long term. Such decisions can come with a huge cost, affecting one's job, marriage and social life.

Doing nothing about such feelings can have repercussions. According to a 2012 *Forbes* magazine article, the sense of "feeling boxed in could seriously compromise well-being."[7]

The article, written by Alice G. Walton, also noted that middle-aged men today are sandwiched in between two different generations and approaches to conducting one's life, which can add more stress and uncertainty.

It is a cultural quandary, Walton said. On one hand, there are the traditional silent, strong, macho ways of our fathers. On the other, the more progressive, open and self-centered approach to life that we see in our kids. Which way do we go?

Justin Denney, a sociologist at the University of Colorado, has studied the relationship between family structure and suicide rates. Denney and others report that suicide rates are higher among divorced men and lowest among those still married. Single guys fall in the middle.

Interestingly enough, among women, the suicide rates for those married, divorced and widowed are "statistically insignificant."

What gives?

Health experts are divided on the issue, but Denney points out that marriage seems to offer "a support system for men that is uniquely beneficial (to them)."

In an interview, Denney said, "Maybe they forge a relationship and a reliance on their partner that's specific to that relationship. Much as marriage is important to women, it just doesn't seem to be the driving factor."[8]

He said that women just seem to be better at balancing such things as child-rearing responsibilities and employment, while maintaining social connections (friends) outside of their marriage.

That struck a chord with me. My life was out of balance, particularly when it came to male friends. Friendship is like a garden. As any good gardener will tell you, it takes time and care. My friendship garden had not been tended in years. It was full of dead plants, weeds.

After that Annapolis weekend though, things began to change on several fronts.

CHAPTER 5

IT'S NOT ABOUT GETTING A HOBBY

A true friend is someone who thinks that you are a good egg, even though he knows that you are slightly cracked.
~ Bernard Meltzer, radio advice call-in show host

It's the friends you can call up at 4 a.m. that matter.
~ Marlene Dietrich, actress and singer

Who's your best friend?

An appreciable number of married middle-aged men I interviewed responded, "My wife…" but they struggled to come up with a male name when asked to name someone else, apart from her.

Others said they did not have a best friend. They had acquaintances—particularly those men who have moved around and were relative newcomers to a community.

Not all guys, though. Those who have lived in a community for years or never moved away from their childhood homes often had a ready list of names. And others, particularly the divorced guys, readily gave a name or a couple of names—and proceeded to tell me how important these friends were in their lives.

One of the things I have observed with my wife, Laura, (and with many other married women), is that the best friend question often produces the name of another woman. They value their husbands and marriages, but they make additional space for friends on a daily or weekly basis.

As I already said, my wife has a solid group of buddies she plays indoor soccer and softball with, and who she communicates with via email almost daily. Her friends can be, and often are, a sounding board on child-rearing, decorating the house, buying a car, helping to decide where we go out to dinner, landscaping our front yard—you name it. She helps them, they help her.

I sure needed someone to turn to that weekend Laura took off to Annapolis. And I did find someone. But it was not the woman I had been emailing.

That Friday evening, I finally decided to turn around and drive back home. I polished off another couple of beers from the fridge and went to bed, or at least I tried. I tossed and turned all night, wondering if I had made the right decision. I was miserable, bitter toward my wife.

The following morning, the phone rang early. It was my former newspaper editor, David, who had since left journalism and was in the process of writing a book. We had become friends over the years, but we had not been real close in the past couple. I had forgotten I had talked to him earlier in the week and we were supposed to go to a yoga class together at 7:30 a.m. I was having lower-back problems at the time, and yoga seemed to help.

Although I was an absolute wreck that morning from lack of sleep, I went to the class anyway, struggling throughout it. Afterward, David asked if I wanted to go out to breakfast. I agreed.

During breakfast, David noticed I was acting tired, distraught. He asked if there was anything wrong. After beating around the bush for a few moments, I simply blurted out that I thought I might be depressed and that I was thinking about seeing a doctor for help.

As he questioned me further, I began telling him of my frustrations and anger with Laura and her getaways, along with several other issues, including the temptation to have an affair. After listening for a few moments, he convinced me to scrap the visit to the doctor.

"Hell, you're not depressed or losing your mind. You have every right to be pissed at your wife. You're making some good points."

That morning, breakfast was a turning point. We did not solve any problems, but just *talking* about things was a good start. It felt good for both of us. We pledged to each other that we would start getting together for breakfast more often. Deep down though, I knew what I had to do next with Laura. It was not going to be easy.

The Painting Contractor

Al, at age 55, figures he is at the tail-end of middle-age.

"You can kid yourself, but how much more middle can you have? Say by 60, I'll be a senior citizen."

The role of wealth and how it plays out in what one can and cannot do at this stage of life stares him in the face.

"Because you're at the point, or starting to get at the point… you know, some people are *retired* at our age. You hear things like, *Oh, I just went to Africa.* I have a hard time going to Connecticut for the weekend," he said. "It affects your sex life, your emotional health. I talked to a couple last night who went to St. Kitts for two days on a jet. It's like the Rolling Stones or something."

Al said his parents were staunch Roman Catholics. They grew up poor, with a humble, reserved attitude toward life. They considered dancing a pastime of the wealthy.

On the subject of friends, Al recognizes "you need friends more at this age.

"We need them to be connected. I think as men in general, we don't develop the relationships or put the time and effort into it. To me, sports and activities have been real good."

But many of those activities were in years past. Al still referees basketball a lot, partially out of love for the sport and partially out of financial necessity. He has heard other refs talk about the fun things or self-centered things they will be doing with the money they earn. His earnings, he said, have helped pay his family's bills.

Al appeared to be one of those guys who talks the talk, but lately has not been walking the walk.

Asked if he has a best friend, he replied, "You know, I really don't have a strong best friend. I have friends, but I don't have a best friend… I used to."

I followed with a question about who he would call in the event no family members were available for some kind of emergency.

"Maybe one person I could consider like that—maybe, two. I have a brother (who lives on the West Coast). So, I can't really call him. I feel close to him, though."

I asked Al about whether there were any annual, sacrosanct all-guy getaways that he participated in.

"No. Never have. I would like to do an occasional getaway… not a regular thing. Maybe twice a year, or something like that. I'd like to participate, even go somewhere. See a big sports event. Go to a museum. If there was some concert in Washington, D.C., I wouldn't mind that. I hope it would happen. I don't know if it ever will."

The Real Estate Agent

Bill works from an office at his home. I visited him there one evening.

"The 40s seemed to be some kind of weird transition," he said. "I used to play soccer when the kids were small. Now that the kids are in their 20s, a lot of things have changed. I don't know, maybe I'm looking at the back side (of life).

"I feel like there're certain things I want to accomplish, and I'm running out of time. So I feel I need to do something now, or I just won't do them. If I don't take that course, get that certification, then I won't do that."

On the subject of friends, Bill responded, "It's funny, apart from my wife, I don't necessarily have a best friend that I can say. I have a few people who I've stayed in touch with all my life. Every two years, we might get together, talk or email."

I asked him what he would do if his wife was no longer in the picture as a result of divorce or death. He did not answer the question, responding instead that his life was keeping him occupied.

"I'll be honest, I talk to lots of people all the time. I don't have one person. And it changes. They fade out. I get busy doing other stuff."

During his 30s and much of his 40s, Bill said he and his wife had a number of friends and several activities going on outside his marriage.

"We used to hang out. I was in this over-30s soccer league. Used to be friends with a number of guys there. There were also a bunch of families, we got together each year and did the Great Race (a four-person, team triathlon with a runner, biker and two canoeists). And volleyball as we got older. As our careers and family demands became more encompassing, we began going in other directions."

Bill talked about a group he played cards with.

"Whoever was dealing got to call the game. We used to stay up all night. But that just petered out..."

And then there was a gourmet dinner club.

"We started out with five couples. One couple got divorced, one couple moved away. It just ended. So we started another. One couple moved away. It's kind of funny. You look at the person on your left, the person on your right—one of those people will be gone by

Christmas. People keep going on. Circumstances change. We don't have a dinner club now."

And he talked about one particular friend he used to cycle with, a buddy who did not give a second thought about just stopping by, having a cup of coffee, making himself comfortable around the house. He liked the company, but things changed.

"I find some guys will turn you down. Some guys will be real competitive. It all depends on what your goals are. Yeah, you want to go around the lake (cycling). The next thing you know, you're hammering, racing. That wasn't what I wanted to do. So I didn't do it."

He emphasized that many men are too competitive for their own good. That it is hard for them to participate in a sporting activity (in middle age) for the sole purpose of staying socially connected.

"To say it doesn't matter if I win or lose, that I'm just having fun playing this game with you," he said. "It's 'If I can (just) make that winning shot…' That's the nature of men, after a lifetime of doing that."

Lately, he has been looking at things he and his wife share and thinking about the remainder of life. For him, he has taken dancing lessons with her. For her, she is participating in dog agility classes that he has started with their dog. He also talked about an artistic endeavor he has been dabbling in, and would like to continue.

"I've been modeling and making casts of gargoyles. It's funny. I probably have a picture of every gargoyle in Syracuse. Also, pictures of them from Ecuador… Europe, when we visited there. Once in Germany, I went right up to the building, smashed some clay against it and took a reverse mold."

Asked about the satisfaction of his needs in life, Bill prefers the role of the dutiful father, who puts everyone in front of himself. Taking out time for himself—taking time for an all-male getaway—is just not happening.

"I could stand to be selfish, more assertive on the things I want to do. I want to support my family," he said. "If everyone is happy, I'm happy."

Along the way the push and the need to have outside friends and activities has faded.

"As we get older, a lot of things I'm thinking about what I want to do... I assume it'll be with my wife." And the need to connect with other men?

"I think a lot of men invest a lot of time in their wives and marriage. Tend to do more of the working. They're the bread-winners. A lot of demands are on them. It's the nature of women to be more outgoing and gregarious. Social. That's what's behind women maintaining their friendships (as opposed to men). It's sad, but true."

The Insurance Man

Friends told me about Hugh, a divorced guy who, in a way, is kind of legend among certain circles in a nearby community. Here is a guy, 50 years old, divorced with two children living with him, who is routinely dating attractive younger women—many in their early and mid-20s, and is somehow managing to keep it all together.

He said his dating activities have prompted other guys to tell him they have been living "vicariously through me."

"It just happens. I'm not looking for it. Friday night, I was out with a 22-year-old. Saturday, I was out with a 36-year-old," he said. "It's because there are a lot of people who aren't like that at age 50. I'm kind of reversing things. I feel like I'm in my second childhood."

Hugh said he used to "live to work," often taking his vacations at home, but that has changed in recent years. "You can only clean the house so much."

He said he has taken his kids on numerous vacations, and that his top responsibility now is to "make them be happy. And I want to be happy along with them."

I asked, "Just what do younger women see in you?"

"I'm going out with the younger ones now, because they don't want to get married right away. I've dated older women with kids, but I'm not ready to do the *Brady Bunch* thing."

Hugh said the biggest thing with younger women going out with older men is security, along with the financial benefits.

"It's not Sugar Daddy-type stuff like, *Will you buy me a car?* For a lot of them, going out to dinner (with a guy their age) is Applebee's. For me, when I take someone out to dinner, I go to Syracuse—even Rochester.

"A night out with a 21-year-old guy is going to his house and playing video games. A night with me is—I'll take them down to New York City for the weekend."

I asked him if he ever gets lonely.

"We always look at lonely as not having a mate. I'm lonely when my kids are not around for a day or two."

So who does he turn to?

"My friends. They're there. They call me every day. For example, I have one who's a single parent, just like me. And another who's not even divorced. He (the married guy) calls me because he's lonely. I try to keep busy."

Busy? We're talking about three softball teams, a touch football team, and a poker club he has been involved with for 30 years.

"Just about every Sunday, we usually start around 6:30 p.m. and are home by 10:30 p.m.," he said of the poker club. "We used to rotate the games around each week, but one member built a basement just so we could play cards. We're from all stations of life. Half of us are single, and half of us aren't."

I asked Hugh about his 50th birthday. For some guys I talked to, it was not even celebrated. Not this guy.

"It was just a party for me. We've done that (with all the guys in our poker club) when they turned 50—one in

January, one in February, one in March, one in April—dinner, staying out all night."

He said his poker buddies have been there for him in other ways, too. "Everyone has bad moments. We've talked a lot about marriage problems with each other. One person will be having a problem with his wife. The next thing you know, all of us will know about it and call and (offer) support. Let's go out and have a couple of beers and talk over things. There's nothing wrong with hugging a guy once in a while. It's not weird."

Afterthoughts

In her 1995 book, *The New Passages*, author/researcher Gail Sheehy summed up the need for men to have friends and to connect more with others during middle age. She described it as *an essential task*.

"The happiest men move from devoting most of their energy to competing and sexual conquest to devoting more and more of their energy to finding emotional intimacy, trust, and companionship and community with others," she said.[9]

My wife works at a medical equipment manufacturer and each month employees get a Mayo Clinic Health Solutions bulletin, with all sorts of useful health and diet tips. One article in particular, *Why Men Need Friends*, caught my eye.

"Think friendship is just for women? Think again," the article began.

"Although some men aren't aware of the importance of social support, there are significant benefits of friendship on their mental, emotional and physical health," the article continued. [10]

It went on to note how friendships "can take root in common areas, such as work, playing on a sports team or becoming a father." It proceeded to give advice about building and strengthening friendships.

Tips included making time for friendships to develop, sharing information and experiences with other guys, keeping in touch with them through emails and phone calls and getting a group of men together every year for some kind of all-guy outing, such as a camping or skiing trip.

I initially found this amusing, but I suddenly realized it was sad that men had to be reminded of this.

There are a number of middle-aged men out there—I counted myself among them before I started this book—in denial when it comes to understanding the importance and advantages of having and maintaining good, close male friends.

Don't get me wrong. There are many guys who *get it.* Guys who get together regularly in sports leagues, poker clubs, service clubs and church activities that involve social time with other men. Guys who get together every week or every couple of weeks for lunch or breakfast with others, or meet for beers at a local bar. Men who get away annually with others for all-male getaways—hunting trips, camping trips, fishing trips, golf weekends, you name it.

However, there are also a large number of guys who will look you squarely in the eyes and say they do not have, or even see the need for a best guy friend. They avoid putting themselves in a situation where they will spend any significant time with another guy to talk about something heavy or personal.

They have no one they can call on a moment's notice, if they are suddenly confronted with a personal emergency, or if they need help in a home repair job.

These guys lack balance in their lives. If you look at the high rate of depression among our male ranks during middle age, I would bet money that "lack of male friends" figures heavily into it all.

Unsure whether you fall into this category? Ask the woman who sleeps next to you every night. Better yet, check the family calendar or personal day planner to see how many things are written down that entail time with male friends. If the answer is nothing—absolutely nothing—your life is out of balance. Mine sure as hell was.

Wayne, the owner of a local fly fishing shop, who organizes a series of annual fly fishing trips each year to such places as the Florida Keys, Montana or Idaho, told me it is surprising how many men go on these trips as a result of gifts from their wives or girlfriends.

He said many men put everyone else ahead of themselves. "And sometimes, there's something left over for Dad."

I decided to stop feeling sorry for myself. I had to get off my ass, stop whining and reach out to other guys if I wanted to have friends. I began by posting a note card on my bathroom mirror. It is still there today.

It reads, *It won't happen unless I do it.*

That started me on the right track… More on that later.

CHAPTER 6

SPILLING YOUR GUTS

What we have here is failure to communicate.
~ From the movie, "Cool Hand Luke"

The way we communicate with others and with ourselves ultimately determines the quality of our lives.
~ Tony Robbins, life coach, self-help author and motivational speaker

A decision to have an affair, or even to be thinking seriously about one, does not happen overnight.

Think of a camp fire. You stop feeding it wood and it burns down as you hit the sack in your tent or camper. But often, during the course of the night, somewhere among the ashes, a hot, glowing ember remains. Let a little wind come along and it begins to smoke and glow.

And when the situation is right—say, when a napkin, small twigs or leaf is put on the fire the next morning—smoke and sometimes a flame result. I had a few burning embers inside of me.

It is hardly the thing you would bring up with your wife and kids. But like I have already stated, they were seeing the signs: I was yelling, laying blame, flying off the handle more—in their minds, often for no good reason. My wife and children would often side against me when I started to vent about things. I felt disrespected.

The resentment, the frustration, the loneliness kept building inside. Then the Annapolis weekend came. I was primed to make a decision.

That breakfast with my friend David, however, was the nudge back in the right direction that I needed. It emboldened me to seek an alternative course.

When Laura came home that Sunday, she was home for less than an hour before I started in—asking her how much money she had spent, why this was now going to be an annual thing and how my weekend was terrible. She got worked up, I got worked up. We both started shouting at each other. The discussion was going nowhere.

The time had arrived to be honest, to connect the dots.

"I'm thinking of having an affair," I blurted out. I added that the opportunity was staring me right in the face. I told her about the non-stop emails and text messages, and about how the whole thing was tearing my guts out.

"And that's supposed to make me feel better?" she responded, lips quivering, tears streaming down her cheeks.

The Pilot

Sky, 51, is divorced, but currently in a serious relationship with a woman he really loves.

On the subject of communication, he said, "Men are good communicators, when the women give them a chance. Some guys are, some guys aren't. But the subject can have a lot to do with that. A lot of guys in a lot of subject areas tend to just clam up, until they're put in the right situation and then they become this fountain of information."

He talked about how he met his girlfriend on a ski trip. How they met one night in the hot tub at a motel they were staying at and ended up making out. But when it came to making any further moves in the days to follow, he froze.

"I was sitting in a bar (a few days later), talking to this flight attendant about this, and she said, Just call her up. I told her, I can't do that. What the hell am I going to say?" She said, "Don't worry. Just call her. That's what girls like." So he called her. On the phone, he said, the words just poured out.

"We went out a couple of times, just talking about life, this thing and the other thing… I felt like, you know what? My last wife and I never talked about things."

He emphasized that listening is important—on both ends of a relationship.

"Sometimes putting a label on a guy who doesn't communicate is because… maybe he's not being listened to patiently and with compassion about what he's trying to get across."

The Accountant

Sam, 49, readily admits he has his strengths and weaknesses when communicating. He discussed his difficulty in conversing with women.

"I can explain things well. But I'm not good at explaining my feelings. I'm terrible, I'm the worst."

He feels that women are just too emotional.

"Everything is tied to an emotion," he said. "Just having a disagreement with someone creates an emotional imprint. That emotional imprint gets brought back, brought back, brought back. They can't get over things."

There is something else. Many just "can't bury the hatchet," he added. "I see it with my wife, with women I work with. They just can't give it up. You have an argument with your wife, you go to bed and you wake up in the morning. You think it's over. It's not."

The Painting Contractor

Al, 55, said genetics may play a factor in the differences of how men and women communicate.

"I think women are more highly evolved creatures in the whole evolutionary chain. Especially in terms of expressing themselves and being in touch with their feelings. I absolutely feel they're at a higher level."

I asked him to be more specific.

"They listen to what the others have to say. They seem more in tune to non-verbal cues. They're more sensitive to colors, shades, lightings. The strength of responses are more important to them than they are to us. Not all women, not all men. But by far, most. That's certainly a strength of women and a weakness of men."

The Police Officer

David, 48, said up until recently his habit of keeping things to himself concerning his marriage has been a problem over the years.

"To me, the less I said, I felt the better off things would be. It wasn't true. The less I said, the worse it got. I've since learned to open up and communicate more.

"I think what a lot of men can learn from women is that no matter what you say, as long as it's done respectfully and there's open dialogue to get to the end result, that's the best you can do. Because not doing that, you know, keeping your feelings inside… I mean, the tension just remains."

The Counselor

Mike, 55, believes men could learn from women, and women from men.

"The key thing is women seem to feel less threatened with self-disclosure. But for men, we really didn't grow up with that. That's not part of our culture. On top of that, we (as men) don't support one another in self-disclosure. So it's hard."

He continued along that line, adding, "Women invite men to do self-disclosure, but women have the advantage of learning to do that with other women."

Mike said in general, "Women with their better verbal acuity tend to dominate a man and use that to their advantage. I think probably men need to know their frustrations in conversations (with women) are not without basis."

I told him that when I first started researching for this book, I was told by several women that I would never get the truth from men, that their wife or girlfriend should sit in on the interview. But after three interviews with couples, I became frustrated and gave up on that approach. The women did more than 75 percent of the talking.

Mike smiled.

"Which came first? That men never speak, or the other side of the coin—that they don't get any space?" he asked. "That's an observation. Men get cut off and women go off and are talking among themselves about things."

Afterthoughts

After leveling with Laura, one thing became clear. Neither of us had a ready answer, a solution for how to mend things. One thing we both agreed upon: things were tattered and we needed marriage counseling.

We decided to see a counselor together. Others choose to meet separately. Frankly, I wanted to hear what she had to say to an independent third party—and the reaction she got. I am sure she felt the same about me.

What I ended up bringing into those counseling sessions was a list of gripes, all my resentments. I referred to them as "notes on slips of paper in my pocket." I had lots of them. And the surprising part (for me) was Laura was clueless on many of them, or felt they had been handled long ago.

The counselor set the ground rules. We would cover our issues, resolving them one at a time. We agreed as each one was handled, we would move on to the next and not go back on ground we had already covered.

The approach proved effective.

It had gotten to the point where nearly every time I threw a tantrum there were all these underlying and unspoken issues—issues that neither my wife nor kids were aware of.

At such times, I would spiral out of control. I would stop talking about the issue at hand and begin ranting about not getting any respect. Laura would simply shut me down, or walk away from me. This scenario kept playing out in front of the kids.

The counselor helped us sort all this out, making us both aware of what I was doing—what we were doing to each other.

We talked about how Laura did not give it a second thought when I told her I was getting together with the woman from my past whom I had dated.

"Do you realize how naïve you were?" the counselor asked Laura.

It hurt to see her cry, reinforcing that I still cared very deeply for her. Meanwhile, I was embarrassed to have her lay out how I was so consumed about my own work and that I rarely, if ever, showed interest or concern about what she was going through at hers.

"You never listen or want to listen to me," she said.

We talked extensively about our finances, about how I was spending less and less on myself, and how Laura was going the other way with her friends. And most important, we covered how we were spending less money and time doing things together.

The subject of sex (and lack of) received a fair hearing. We noted our 25th anniversary was coming up and nothing was planned. The counselor recommended an overnight getaway, something we had not done in a few years. We agreed.

Several weeks later in the car, as we drove to the hotel that weekend, Laura became uncomfortably quiet, despondent. At one point, her eyes got red and teary as she quietly looked out the window. I pulled the car over.

She said it had gotten to the point where she did not know what I expected from her anymore—as a wife, as a lover.

It was a pivotal moment.

I told her the most beautiful part of every morning and night—the time I look forward to more than anything else each day—is the time when we cuddle in bed. It is at those times, I said, that nothing else seems to matter.

It was the right answer. We had no problem communicating the rest of the weekend.

CHAPTER 7

GETTING IT ON – OR NOT

See, the problem is that God gives men a brain and a penis, and only enough blood to run one at a time.
~ Robin Williams, comedian

Anybody who believes that the way to a man's heart is through his stomach flunked geography.
~ Robert Byrne, author and well-known pool player

Lots of funny things have been written about sex.

It is no laughing matter, though, when you are a middle-aged guy and getting very little sex—or have been going cold turkey for months, even a year (or years) at a time because of an uninterested mate or other issues.

For me, sex is absolutely necessary in middle age. It was on one of those slips of paper I kept pulling out of my pocket during our marriage counseling sessions.

I know there are plenty of sexless, or relatively sexless married couples and individuals out there. Maybe it is hormones, or the lack thereof. Other reasons frequently cited include lack of time, lack of passion, or the absence of a relationship that once was.

I am not about to pass judgment. One size does not fit all. And if couples are happy doing what they are doing (or not doing), who am I to say what is right or wrong?

For me, at this stage of my life, it is a crucial element of my marriage. A 53-year-old architect I interviewed said he and his wife had recently discussed the need for sex in their relationship. It went beyond just satisfying personal needs.

"When we first married, I was attracted to this woman. There was passion… and a lot of it was physical, as well as emotional. I think you have to maintain that (at some level) in order to sustain your relationship. Otherwise, you're just sort of cohabitating."

When I turned 50, it was not like Laura and I were never having sex. But the frequency was getting less and less and I was initiating it 99 percent of the time. More often than not, our lovemaking was ill-timed, rushed and frequently unsatisfying for both of us.

I was reading all sorts of bad things into refusals or her ambivalence—lack of love, lack of respect, and lack of physical attraction. I am, and have always been, a very physical and touchy person. If I go more than three weeks without getting something—anything—I start getting a little squirrelly.

Laura conceded during our counseling that it was not all in my head—that in recent years her sex drive had diminished, the result of menopause and resulting hormonal changes. Add to that a pre-occupation with other things (the kids, work, finances, friends, etc.).

She had told me all this before—that she sometimes just did not feel like having sex, and that I should not read into it. That is easier said than done.

A healthy sex life, or any sex life for that matter, does not just happen. It is dependent on other things being in alignment in a relationship.

When I hear of a guy leaving his wife because of lack of sex, or vice versa, I have to believe I am not hearing the whole story. A bad sex life is often symptomatic of other problems in a relationship—particularly poor communication and selfishness.

The Retail Manager

Jeremy is a 52-year-old widower. He had been married for years and despite temptations said he had always remained true to his wife. The latter years of the marriage had been difficult, though, as she struggled with a chronic disease. He said when his wife initially found out about her illness, she told Jeremy that he should go find someone else.

"She said we ought to break up. That she's got this disease and it's only going to get worse. That now's my time to get out."

He responded that if she ever did that to him, "that would be an insult. I told her I was into this for the long haul."

The day she died in the hospital, he remembers going into her room by himself to say goodbye.

"It was one of the toughest things I've ever done in my life. She was dead. I bent over and kissed her. You know, I don't have no regrets. What doesn't kill you makes you stronger. Life knocks you down. You just have to get up and keep going."

Less than a year after her death, Jeremy started tapping into the computer dating scene. When his wife was sick, Jeremy said he was lucky if he had sex a couple of times during the year. The computer dating scene was completely different.

"Let me tell you. There are two types of people out there," he said. "Some who are really sincere and others who are players. All they're out to do is to go bang someone. That's all they want. Nothing else."

A friend who got Jeremy into the computer dating scene told Jeremy that before he got married he went out with 66 different women whom he met on the Internet.

"He said he had one coming in the morning and another in the afternoon… that's a player."

Jeremy said when he first contemplated dating he did so out of loneliness. One day he drove to a nearby city and spent the afternoon stopping in one store after another hoping to meet someone, to run into someone he knew.

He soon realized computer dating was a much quicker method.

Before long, he found himself online on three or four dating websites, spending several hours a night.

"You basically put your bio and picture up there (some people don't do the picture). I put mine up and like to see others. You know, most people judge a book by its cover."

The results were immediate. However, he realized, "although a lot of guys aren't angels, there's so many head cases out there who are women."

Some women he met were more conservative, careful and not ready to hop in bed right away. Others were. He told of meeting with a local nursery school teacher, "who looked drop-dead gorgeous—like Carly Simon. She had freaking long legs. She belonged in *Playboy*." He arranged to meet her at a local mall.

They sat down to talk on a bench. The conversation revealed she was getting divorced.

"We're sitting there talking, and suddenly she opens her jacket and has this low-cut thing on," he said. "She started messing around, pulling her shirt down… and asks me, 'Did you bring your truck? I'd really like to get you in your truck.'"

So they start walking toward the truck, and she suddenly pulled Jeremy aside at the mall entrance.

"She throws her tongue down my throat at the mall entrance with people walking by. But there was something inside of me that said, *No, I don't do this*. I quickly said, *Okay, I got to go*, and I just quit talking to her. But oh my God, she had a freaking great body."

He related other stories, such as the women who wanted to get it on in the back of a movie theater and the one who wanted to do it right out in the middle of the lake on his bass fishing boat.

"Not all are like that, but some are very sexually aggressive," he said. He talked about one date that ended up in bed at night's end and how afterward he heard a very unsettling rumor—that she was intent on sleeping with 30 guys in 30 days. He never called her back.

He said he keeps telling himself he is going to find "someone decent. I hope I don't wait until I'm 65 to get back into a solid relationship."

Jeremy, who said he believes in God, has an attitude that everything has a purpose. It comes from a poem that his wife's best friend sent to him after she passed away.

"Women come into your life for a reason, a season—or a lifetime. It's a pretty cool poem and there's truth in it."

The Middle School Teacher

Vic, 55, is in his second marriage. He looks at himself as being "in the middle of my middle age." He casts a critical eye at other guys who are in their mid-50s "and don't have the health, the vitality, the desire to do a lot of things. I have a lot of friends who aren't happy," he said.

"They're waiting to retire, sitting on their butts and doing nothing. That's a pretty sad state of affairs. They're 55 going on 70. That's a pretty accurate way to put it."

He has been physically active most of his life by running and playing basketball. However, he nearly died of a heart attack in his mid-40s.

"They put the paddles on me. You wake with all those tubes, the white lights… other stuff. It was quite scary. I'm walking around right now with a defibrillator in me."

Vic said the heart attack was a defining moment of middle age, along with one other thing: erectile dysfunction.

"I had this mid-life crisis. It was when I was 50-51. It was like oh-oh, the old boy is not working. It was the first time I truly realized I was hitting middle age and questioned my youth. I can't remember the exact date or time, but I do remember thinking it's not supposed to be like this. I realized I needed to seriously consider taking *Viagra*."

Vic said he has never had problems before, or between his first and second marriages, which he described as "a pretty promiscuous time."

He married a younger wife and feels that sex is "absolutely necessary" in his life. "You need a physical relationship. It's just not the intercourse and climax. You need it to feel good, to have that closeness in a relationship."

When asked if his wife feels different about the importance of sex, he responded, "My attitude is we have five minutes, let's go do it. We have five hours, let's go do it a few more times. My wife's attitude is okay… most of the time."

I asked him if he ever keeps any kind of score, or thinks about how much sex he is having—or not.

"Yeah, I keep score in some imaginary scoreboard in the back of my head. I look at my performance. Thank God for medication. It's proven to be a life saver."

The Web Page Designer

Ian, who is twice divorced, said his attitude toward life boils down to: "I'm taking things as they come. I'm not overly concerned."

When I talked to him, he was 10 days shy of his 50th birthday. He had no plans to celebrate.

Ian puts a strong emphasis on his physical conditioning, noting he could run farther and faster and lift more weights now compared to when he was younger.

He said he has dated a wide variety of women. They were younger, his age, slightly older, but mostly younger.

"I wasn't looking for younger women. They found me. There's a lot of women attracted to older men. They're tired of dealing with youngsters. They just feel they're not getting anywhere with guys they got. They're attracted to older guys, who are more settled, not partying all the time or chasing other people."

Does he find sex different in middle age?

"Yeah, we make an appointment for it," he laughed.

I asked him if sex is more important for men than women.

"I think sex for a woman is even more important, from my experiences. I think as women get older they become not afraid to explore their bodies and not afraid to ask for what they want. They're actually more aggressive than when they're younger."

He said as men get older "we tend to mellow out more."

"I think it's a dirty trick. When we were younger, testosterone levels were a lot higher and you're ready to go on a moment's notice. We get a little bit older, it almost shifts. You see the women blossoming and going out, heading up committees. It's very similar with their sex lives. They're raring to go."

The Small Business Owner

Jim, 50, is twice divorced. He is living with a woman in her mid-40s and in no hurry to get married again.

On the subject of sex, "It's not nearly as necessary as it was when you're younger. I think the basic urges are not as strong. Obviously, we're all much older and much fatter," he laughed.

Nevertheless, he added, it is still part of having a close relationship. It enhances the bond. But experience has shown that it can have "an unfortunate side," in that its importance to men "makes it a very useful manipulative tool" for women.

"My second divorce was not a pretty one. There was a lot of shit that went down that hopefully she'll burn in hell over," he said. "I just hope I can watch."

In his current relationship, his impression is that his girlfriend does not "see (sex) as quite as important."

There's a lot of things going on in her life, he said. She works a full-time and has a couple of children.

"She probably puts in a longer week than I do. For most women, especially if they have kids, there's this crescendo of responsibility during this time."

He added, "Once the kids break off, then I think the opportunities open up. You talk about women kind of blossoming. That kind of comes in. That's on the assumption they don't try to refill the nest in one way or another. I've seen a lot of families, though, where there are 25-year-old kids still living at home."

The Police Officer

David said sex plays a major role in his marriage. But there are differences in their attitudes—in part due to the differences between men and women, and also because his wife has just entered menopause.

"I just read a book this morning about women in menopause so I can handle what she's going through," he said. "Lately, it's been like, *What's wrong?* and she says she's having a hot flash. I needed to read up on it so I can understand."

David, 48, said sex "fulfills" the connection between himself and his wife, but that often they view the process differently.

"Women feel that there's this whole process they need to go through in order to be intimate, and that men just want to have sex to get that urge satisfied."

He acknowledged that his wife's plate is "often full" with work and taking care of the kids and at the end of the day after "juggling so many things" she's often exhausted.

David said she has told him he just wants to have sex, but she wants to make love and that there is a difference between that. She says there is nothing wrong with that, and sometimes she wants to just have sex, too. But that I have no idea what goes through her mind during the course of a day.

He was watching Oprah on TV recently and the subject was why men and women are not having sex. "They (the women) were saying basically the same thing my wife is saying… it's just men want to get on top of you and do their thing and that's it. That for us (women) it's a whole process and that men just don't understand that."

What amazed him, though, was "all the women in the audience" who raised their hand who are not having sex.

I asked him about whether he has ever given thought about his sexual prowess in middle age.

"Yeah, you know, you see all those commercials on TV about erectile dysfunction and you think about it. But it goes on to say if you have an erection for more than four hours, go see a doctor."

Regardless, he has contemplated trying *Viagra* or some other drug, noting his erections do not last as long as when he was "in his prime."

"My wife says that's all I think about. But sometimes it's like, *Dang, that was kind of quick*, and I think, *That it couldn't have been good for you*," he said.

David smiled while recalling a line from comedian Bernie Mac.

"He said, 'You know what? When I'm having sex, the first thing I tell my wife is look, I have three good minutes in me. I'll go get mine, you better get yours.'"

The Store Owner

Simon, 52, said sex is not a priority for his wife. She is busy with the kids, taking care of the house and other things.

"I know folks who tell me they still have an active and enjoyable sex life in their 50s, but more people I talk to do not. I know a lot of women friends who are fairly frank about their situation and also feel that they've grown apart from their spouses."

What is common, he said, "is that a lot of guys have given up on it… accepted it. Let's put it that way."

Is he happy with the amount of sex he is getting in his marriage?

"If you're talking about performance-wise or climaxing, I'm pretty much of the opinion is that any sex is good sex. There's no such thing as a bad blow job."

Does he keep score?

"I'll say, jeez, it's been three, four or five months," Simon said. "She'll say no. I'll say bullshit. I know when it last was. After a while, it comes down to why bother. And I know a lot of guys who would agree, or least have a similar situation."

Sometimes he wonders when he hears about couples with healthy sex lives… that maybe it is not because the husband ended up with "a hot-looking wife." Maybe it is a matter of chance and choice.

"You think, maybe you just want one that's horny and you think that maybe you made a mistake," he said. "Maybe I should have gotten the big girl that really wasn't so attractive, but she really, really likes to have sex all the time. And who cares what she looks like at the Christmas party and that sort of thing."

Simon said it would behoove women to understand and appreciate "that most guys, including myself, find certain types of sex more enjoyable. And that if you know what he likes, yeah, you go ahead. What's the big deal? You know, there's a lot of things both people do that they may not be ecstatic about, but you know, you're not doing it for you. You're doing it for him."

He said it is sad, but he knows of men who have "very active sex lives," but it is not with their wives.

"I believe most guys I know want to have sex and are going to find a way to have it, either by themselves or with someone. If it's not happening at home, it's going to happen with a prostitute, a girlfriend or something."

Simon said women are "kidding themselves" that their husbands can absolutely abstain from sex for lengthy periods of time and not look elsewhere.

"And maybe the guys are fooling themselves that the women don't care. I always tell my wife if you can find a boyfriend that's going to take care of it, go for it. Because if you're so damn miserable, maybe that will make you happy."

Afterthoughts

Getting back to the concept of alternative universes, I was not surprised when most married men I talked to said that they wanted sex more than their wives did.

However, I was stunned to hear from divorced or single guys that they are frequently encountering the exact opposite out on the dating scene. They said middle-aged women are often more sexually aggressive and demanding than they are, and in many cases do not want, or need commitment.

Several men I talked to described the growing number of women out there who are players (sexually), along with those who are seeking "sex buddies" (also called *friends with benefits*)—namely men they can date occasionally, sleep with, and then return unattached to the support system of their full-time jobs, their girlfriends, family or to a single parent situation that they do not want to complicate or muck up.

In her 2003 book, *Sex and the Seasoned Woman*, Gail Sheehy noted her research found more than enough evidence to confirm what these guys told me: That there is a "surge of vitality in women's sex and love lives after 50 (both inside and outside of marriage)… a new universe of passionate, liberated women… who are unwilling to settle for the stereotypical roles of middle age" [11]

She likened the phenomenon to a "cultural tsunami."

One woman I talked to about this noted that middle-aged women are also aware of the competition, namely younger women. If they find a man who is decent, who fits the bill of what they are looking for, sex sooner than later can help "seal the deal." They don't want to waste time. Or if nothing else, it keeps him interested, she said.

These are gross generalizations. Of course, it is not all, or every woman. I cannot give you a percentage. However, the trend of sex playing a strong role in the lives of middle-aged women is definitely out there.

If that is the story on the singles scene, what is the lowdown for us married guys?

I can just talk about me. I am married to a woman who is smack dab in the middle of menopausal change, who is embracing her new life as an empty nester, throwing herself into her career—along with connecting and reconnecting with female friends.

And during her pursuit of the passionate life, I have come to realize she does not want to return to the caretaker role of the child-rearing years (always taking care of the kids and me). She is looking for a marriage that involves a mutually supporting, loving partner, a partner she can enjoy the second half of her life with.

Once I accepted all that, our relationship took a turn for the better.

So, what about sex?

My wife and I got a kick a few years ago as we both read an unauthorized biography of Mick Jagger. In it, Jerri Hall, the rocker's then-wife, was asked how she kept the lead singer of the Rolling Stones satisfied in the bedroom, and kept him from cheating on her while he was on the road. Her reply was lots of sex—specifically giving him a blow job or a hand job every opportunity she got. [12]

That's one titillating solution, but hardly practical for us regular middle-aged guys with regular jobs.

In the end, Jagger's insatiable libido and other diversions in his life contributed to breaking up their marriage. Hall did manage, though, to hold on to him longer than any other woman whom he had been with up to that point. Maybe there was some sort of life lesson there.

If you decide you want a lively and satisfying sex life, all I can say is it pays to talk it out with your significant other and listen closely to what each other's needs are. And damn it, be blunt and put things into action. When communication lines open up, you won't always get what you want, but like Jagger, you'll get what you need.

Do I lovingly serve Laura coffee and give her the newspaper in bed each morning? You are darn right I do! And does she grant my occasional wish when she is up reading late to wake me for some *late night delight* before she finally nods off?

Not always, but often enough.

CHAPTER 8

THE YOUNGER WOMAN THING

I've reached the age where competence is a turn-on.
~ Billy Joel, musician, song writer

I always say now that I'm in my blonde years. Because since the end of my marriage, all my girlfriends have been blonde.
~ Hugh Hefner, publisher, founder of *Playboy* magazine

Married men have affairs—or at least strongly consider them—for a variety of reasons.

There is this stereotype out there that men are just pigs and that when they tire of, or are no longer having satisfactory sex with their current mates, they toss them aside for younger, sexier women.

I am not denying that the older man/younger woman phenomenon is widespread. But I feel that a lot of men's middle age crises—specifically involving decisions to embark on an affair—are a helluva lot more complicated than just wanting to bed a younger babe.

As for the younger women thing, I never felt the urge, but one never knows. The opportunity never arose. The reality was that I still physically craved my wife, who is a year younger than I am. Even when we were having problems, I still looked her over longingly as she got out of the shower or got dressed. Still do.

My conversations with married and single middle-aged men on the topic raised more questions than were answered. Do middle-aged men, if given the chance, naturally gravitate toward younger women? Or, as one divorced guy noted, was I asking the wrong question?

"You should be asking why younger women gravitate toward older men," he said.

The Lawyer

Tony, 47, said this whole thing about all men always gravitating toward younger women is "total horseshit—although, when you come to think about it, a lot of guys we know have picked up with younger women."

"If I get a second shot, I'm taking whatever came my way that I was interested in, and wouldn't necessarily go looking for a younger woman," he said, adding that the most important thing is finding someone he could "connect with mentally, emotionally and physically."

He said guys who focus exclusively on younger women are insecure about their own death, are insecure about that woman in their life who left them… and they are now wondering, *Is there something wrong with me?*

"A younger woman would have more of a tendency to put (the guy) up on a pedestal than someone their own age."

And finally, he said, you will see a middle-aged man go out with a younger woman, "because he knows when he goes out, he'll be well thought of by other guys."

Tony recalled this cartoon he once saw that showed how men and women look at themselves differently in the mirror.

"You have a beautiful woman that looks in the mirror and all she can see is a fat woman who can't wear a two-piece bathing suit. And you see this fat, balding guy who looks in the mirror and he thinks he's Adonis. Guys think of themselves on a higher plane… and then maybe they then go looking for someone who matches that. Women tend to be more honest (about things like that)."

Tony said it always bugs him when women see guys with younger women and immediately begin voicing disapproval. "It's tantamount to marrying a sister in their eyes."

He mentioned how a guy he knew showed up at a youth hockey tournament he was at with his son and a "significantly younger woman by his side."

"I found her to be intelligent and a pleasure to have a conversation with," he said.

However, the reaction "from every woman I know, including the former wife was, 'Have you seen the trollop he's going out with now?'"

Tony said none of these women knew her or took the time to talk to her. She is labeled, though as "the worst thing to be born on earth—all because she's younger.

"She must have violated some female commandment that exists. A commandment that (we guys) are unaware of. It's kind of like the Masons, a secret society."

The Accountant

Sid said for most guys it is true—they want to be with younger women.

"Let's put it this way, everybody wants to be with someone who's attractive and young—and younger people are more attractive than older people. However, personally I think it's a matter of being more in control. Being the person, being the authority… calling the shots. You know what I mean?"

He concedes a lot of older women are "probably on the downside as far as their interest in sex, and so you go for someone younger."

Sid, 49, considers himself among the exceptions since he married a woman 10 years older.

"If I was going to have an affair with someone, it would be with someone older… not my age or younger," he said. "It's probably just a mental thing. Mentally being in tune with somebody. Even though I consider myself younger and things like that, from a mental maturity standpoint, I'm an older person."

The Entertainment Manager

Steve, 55, said his first marriage ended following mistakes and immaturity by both himself and his wife. "I just became an unbelievably stupid jerk-off in my late 30s."

He decided to concentrate afterward on his career and being true to his ideals. A magazine article he read made a huge impression on him. The advice: Look around and see where you are and see if you can advance the organization you are with to the place you want to be.

He did that and noted he is now happy with his career and life in general. The organization he leads has grown and steadily improved. He sees himself in an enviable position.

"A lot of people do for fun what I do for a living," he smiled.

He described himself today as a middle-aged man who craves and needs sex. "It's just so much who I am, and who I have been since age 18. It's a lot of things. It's a self-esteem thing. I have a tremendous need for physical affection, not necessarily connected to love. I still probably think about sex as much as when I was 18."

Steve remarried about five years ago to a woman who is near his age. "My wife and I both have pronounced libidos. And we're really, really going to be loyal (to each other) this time… And that's both of us."

He said the entertainment business has a constant emphasis on good looks and staying in shape.

"I'm surrounded by men and women who are incredibly sexually active and are until way in life."

I asked him about the younger woman thing.

"For me, it's a total package. I gravitate toward women who attract me, anywhere from in their 20s into their 60s. If I'm going to spend any time with anyone at all, they really have to have an education. I just can't stand there and talk about nothing. But I'm unusual. I'm constantly surrounded by college-educated women of all ages."

His theory about why many men gravitate to younger women boils down to the fact "they've not slept with a lot of women.

"When you've slept with a lot of women, you realize that age is not the defining factor. And you can always say, *naah… she'll be looking in the mirror* (later at her sagging breasts)… *naah, she doesn't know much… naah, she's a waste of time.* Believe me, I've done research."

The Medical Specialist

Phil, 54, has found himself recently in an empty nest situation, with his children off to college.

On the topic of sex, he said, it is important to him. As for his wife, who is slightly younger, "When she wants to have sex, she has sex… I'll never turn her down.

"I'm always into it. It's a male type of thing. If it's breathing, you'll have sex with it. As for menopause, though, I don't have a good read on it."

Phil's read on the younger woman thing is that a younger woman "will facilitate a man to feel younger. To get involved in younger things.

"I don't know if it's a matter of reliving, or reigniting things from way back when. There's romance. All of a sudden you can be young again. You have this young babe. You get a leather coat. It's kind of like a rebirth, or starting over. A redo."

He said men who have affairs in middle age do so often because they are under the impression that "time is running out. They're looking to reignite something in themselves. Something that inwardly they've lost and they want to get back.

"They're in a rut. Maybe it's their ego. If it's their ego, they've probably been having affairs all along. When (we men) hit our 50s and 60s, though, there's a lot of pressure. If you're going to do it, now is the time. If you want that fast car, now's the time. If you want to have an exciting sex life, you want to have it now. It's not going to get any better from here on in."

The Carpenter

Frank has been divorced for 10 years. The 54-year-old said while financially his life "is very unstable," there were two constant things: his desire to stay close and be a good father to his children, and to stay physically in good shape.

As for the children, he said, "There's this guilt, that I could have done more. It still gets me depressed from time to time. That when I left, one of them was still very young. I try to overcome it by being the best I can for now."

On his 50th birthday, Frank ran a difficult, nine-mile cross country race that involved running through woods, corn fields and over creek beds. He was proud of that.

"When I got there, they handed me my number. It was 50, which was really, really significant."

He has had more than his share of women in recent years. He said sex in middle age, though, has become "less necessary than it was" when he was in his 30s and 40s.

It's different for women, he added.

"It becomes an increasingly high priority for women from 39 to late 40s, early 50s. Maybe they seek to be something that's slipping away from them."

He said women look at older men as being "more seasoned, more established" financially and emotionally. During high school his daughters kept telling him that the girls were often more mature than the boys—and that trend often seemed to just continue as they grew older.

Frank remembers "jumping through all sorts of fiery hoops" to get women into bed when he was in his late 30s and early 40s.

"The past five years, I have to work a lot less and I get a lot more offers than when I was running after women like crazy. A lot of times, all I have to do is just show up (at a party, or some kind of social gathering)."

He recalled an incident when he met this medical student ("She was 28 or 29, or something.") at this summer party.

"And I said, *Oh, what a beautiful night!* And then she said, 'Want to go for a drive?' And she pretty much took over from there. I had no idea I was getting any closer than just talking to her."

So Frank drove her to nice place overlooking the city of Syracuse.

"I stopped the car and asked if she wanted to take a walk and continue talking. I truly, truly had no plans, no clue. I hadn't even touched her with my finger."

As they got out of the car and walked a short distance, she suddenly started shedding her clothes.

"She said, 'Do you want to do it in the car, or in the grass?'"

They did it in the grass.

Afterthoughts

Scott, 60, a retired teacher I interviewed, has only been married once. And although there has been a "number of bumps in the road" he said he has stayed the course and never strayed. I asked him about the younger woman thing.

"You see a guy, 60 or 65 walking around with a younger, nice-looking chick. And you say to yourself, *What do they have in common?* It's got to be about the sex. I mean, c'mon. Think about it. You were raised in the 1950s, came of age during the 1960s and you're out with someone who came of age in the Reagan years. No common music, reading… no common anything. I think it would just have to be about the sex."

Susan, a female friend, told me her father had this "older men, younger women" thing down to a formula.

"If given the chance (through divorce or death of a spouse) a man will pick a woman that's half his age, plus seven years," she said.

I asked about the "plus seven" bit and she said it is to provide a comfort zone to ensure the woman is at least older than his daughters.

I do not know about that. All I know is that now being in my late-50s, I look around and see the baggage that comes along with being with a younger woman. I am talking about having to go once again through those child-rearing years. Both my kids are grown and in, or have finished college.

Laura (and I think many married, middle-aged women for that matter) is way ahead on that front. She saw this change coming several years ago and immersed herself in creating close relationships with, and being involved in weekly activities with female friends.

I am trying to catch up. After years of self-sacrifice, of being involved in all the kids' activities and sports, I am all about working on enjoying life more, expanding my career as an outdoors writer—and most of all, working on becoming the best life partner I can possibly be with Laura.

Would I want to go back to all-consuming, diaper-changing/PTA days (and later worry about another round of college loans) just so I can have sex with a younger woman? No way. But that is me.

As I have said repeatedly, there are a number of alternative universes out there. And some guys relish the idea of a Round II (or III) with a family, of getting a second chance at being a parent again because they screwed things up so badly the first time around.

Or, maybe it really is a matter of trading in one model of woman for another sexier model. Or better yet, wanting a woman who understands you, respects you, appreciates you, has fun with you and makes you feel young… and yes, lusts for you on occasion. Is that too much to ask, or to strive for? I don't think so.

I often hear about married middle-aged women saying that as a result of menopause they have a reduced sex drive, or that sex because of dryness down there is uncomfortable for them—that they could do without it much of the time.

My response to these women may sound harsh, but it's food for thought: *Can you do without your marriage?* Not to decide is to decide.

If you have evolved during the childcare years from a marriage with sex to a marriage without, and you have a husband who at times gets horny as hell—what do you expect?

There are a lot of advances in medicine (hormone therapy, creams, etc.) out there for middle-aged women who want to continue having, and enjoying sex.

Of course, good sex is not just about taking pharmaceuticals, which merely enhance things. It comes as a result of a good, healthy, loving, open relationship with your significant other in which you recognize and take care of each other's needs.

I know that some women think of men who gravitate to younger women as being pigs and extremely shallow-minded. But let's turn the tables. What is a younger woman who gravitates to an older, better-off guy? Is she being a superficial swine as well?

The truth is sex and money are not the only things that makes the world go round. Life is more complicated than that. You often hear about guys, though, who take the younger woman route and end up regretful as hell afterward. However, there are numerous examples out there of guys who do it and things work out for the best.

All I know is, I am the best husband, lover and best father I can be when I am happy with myself.

The woman who can help me with that, or at least tries to make that happen—whatever her age—will never have to worry about me looking for someone else.

CHAPTER 9

ANGSTING ABOUT MONEY

I finally know what distinguishes man from other beasts: financial worries.
~ Jules Renard, author

Money is something you got to make in case you don't die.
~ Max Asnas, founder and resident sage at New York's famous Stage Delicatessen

I have never really made much money as a journalist. I never fretted about that until I hit my 50s.

Then the worrying started: about retirement, about college for the kids, about having more than two or three cars (and carrying the insurance for everyone), about the ever-mounting debt that we had accumulated to pay for our lifestyle, our past vacations. Worse yet, worrying about the status of my job—about the newspaper industry in general.

When I hit middle age it was gut check time. Am I earning enough? Is there time to make a change in a career if I wanted, or needed to? More importantly: Can I afford to make a change, particularly with two kids poised to enter college?

Add to all that the week-to-week financial worries. When my wife, who paid all the bills, would say, "Don't spend any more than you have to—things are going to be really, really tight the next couple of weeks," I would get this sick feeling in my stomach.

It has helped that Laura, after years of part-time or lower-paying full-time jobs, embarked in her 40s on a well-paying, full-time job with a career path. It meant more money in our checkbook each week.

In any relationship, though, money is power. The person who makes all, or the majority of it often has the upper hand. But in a dual-income marriage, the one who knows where it is all going is in the driver's seat.

I was pitiful. I had reached middle age and had no idea how Laura was juggling the bills each week. Hell, I did not even know the passwords to check the status of our checking and savings accounts online. All I knew was that my earnings were being directly deposited into our joint checking account each week—and I was clueless about how it was being spent and what our overall status was.

The result was resentment whenever Laura would spend money on herself— particularly activities with her friends. I was spending pittance on myself. That was a big deal with me and was addressed at length during one of our marriage counseling sessions.

The Medical Specialist

With each of my interviews, my walk-away question was always the same. *Is there something you'd like to know more about from other middle-aged guys?* Something I forgot to ask, or I should ask?

Phil, 54, responded that my list of questions ignored the *bogeyman* of today's middle-aged men. It is that tap on your shoulder to meet your boss for a private meeting late Friday afternoon. The unexpected pink slip.

"Let me tell you, I go house to house (with my practice) and I see guys who have been laid off. It's devastating. What do you say to them? What do you do? Especially when someone has given their life to their career.

"You make a joke: *Oh, you can start a second career and everything.* I don't know how it works. You work for a bank for 20 years and get laid off. No bank wants to hire you because you cost too much."

All that creates a lot of pressure on men in today's world. Phil said, it is funny that "there are women's movements, but there's never been a movement for men, of (our age), in this country.

"With the exception of the Million Men March for black guys, we're like ignored."

He mentioned women go through menopause "and it's like I'm hot, I'm cold. Everyone knows. She tells everyone. But there's this guy. He's losing his hair. Getting fatter and everything. Why doesn't he lose some weight? Why doesn't he exercise? Where's the sympathy?

"It's like we're a forgotten segment of the population. Businesses fire us for working too long, making too much money. And now they're cutting all possible benefits for the future… Who's looking out for us?"

Phil said when he was growing up, men worked a lifetime and their company took care of them. But all that has changed.

He talked about one of this brothers who "worked for the Board of Education" and hung in there for his last three years.

"He stuck it out and he was miserable, but he got a great retirement (after retiring at age 56). But my other brother is just like me. I don't think I can ever retire due to the kids and college debt. Everything you read in the paper, it's depressing in terms of spiraling costs, raising tuition. You plan on Social Security kicking in at age 65, but they keep changing the rules."

The Mechanic

Bob, 47, said he is coming to "the mid-point in life where you get to enjoy the fruits of all the labor you did while you were young."

With two grown children, he said he and his wife have a rental property, a cottage on the side of a local lake that they took over from their parents. His wife also has a successful business.

They have both gotten heavily into scuba diving, a passion they share with their children. Several past family vacations have involved trips to exotic locations and diving ventures. They have joined a local diving club.

"We've gotten to be really good friends with a lot of these people," Bob said of the diving club. "They come from all walks of life… from various successful business people, to people who collect garbage on the side of the road."

He said nobody in the club seems to look at each other's material holdings because every time you step into the water, members are looking out for your interests, and you are looking out for theirs. He has not had any doubts about his career path. "I enjoy what I do, interacting with other people."

His wife does all the family's finances.

"My way of thinking is that she goes to work, I go to work. It all goes to one bank, and we're going for one goal. Finances are not an issue with us."

However, he noted there are a lot of relationships in which money is a "big downfall."

"I hear it from a lot of my friends. He has his own checking account; she has her own account. He has his own savings account. That's not a relationship as far as I'm concerned."

His best friend is his wife, followed by his son. He conceded he does not do a lot of things with other guys, other than in the scuba diving club. When he is by himself he likes to dabble in woodworking, "puttering around with various things."

I asked him about spending money on himself, or if he is ever selfish about anything that might *do him some good.*

"I guess for me, being selfish would be to buy things I normally wouldn't buy—like some woodworking tools I normally would pass up. Overall, the thing with me at this point in my life is that material things are not that important to me. If there's something I really want, I'd probably go get it. But I don't yearn for that kind of stuff."

In addition, his belief is that, "Whether you have a million dollars in assets, or a million dollars in tools, when Judgment Day comes you're going to be asked, 'Were you an idiot? Or were you a good person?'"

As for retirement, Bob said, "You have to plan for yourself, and if you depend on Social Security you're nuts. You have to start building assets that one day you know you're going to sell… and you plan."

He said the cottage on the lake is figuring into things.

"We'd like to spend summers there, and go south in the winters. Me, I hate snow. I was born in the wrong climate. The closer I can get to the Equator, the better I'll be."

The Restaurant Owner

Clyde, 50, said his father had a big impact on him. He was always the rock, the head of the family. He was the person who made sure things happened, that the bills got paid and so forth.

"One of the things my dad was very big on was living up to your responsibilities. This was a guy who struggled very hard to support the family, basically making sure those needs were met at any cost. If it ever came down to me wanting to have fun, if say the mortgage payment was in question, that's not acceptable. It just isn't."

Clyde said the relationships men had with their wives a generation ago are different now. Divorces were rare back then, he said. He added when he was in high school, things were just beginning to change in society. Previously, most young women expected to graduate and soon after get married and become housewives. The new emphasis became that "they could have careers. That they should have careers."

As a result, many women in this generation are torn, he said, on how they should lead—or think about—their lives.

"The more feminist people in society are saying there's something wrong with women if they don't have a career."

All this has likewise taken a toll on men, who are torn about how things are supposed to fit together with regard to sex roles.

"For some women, some of the problem is they came into marriages with the mindset that their husband was supposed to look after them because that was the model of their parents. But now, they're in a position where now they have rights. Okay, with rights come responsibilities. That was the scenario with my first wife," he said.

He continued.

"She was 21, but she still had the psyche of a 16-year-old. 'And you know (she said), I don't have to do that. That's old school,'" he said. "Well, I'm sorry, but you're a mother of children. There's something that goes along with that, regardless of what school it is.

"So yeah, it does affect us men," he added.

Clyde emphasized that at times there is a thin line between profit and loss in his business. That calls for him to be constantly "grounded in reality," which he said again presented a problem in his second marriage.

Clyde said the biggest mistake he made with his second wife was having her work in the business with him, and her having access to all the financial accounts. When things went well, it was a joint success. When things went bad, it was his fault.

Then one day, when the going got tough, he said, she just cleaned out their personal and business bank accounts—and left.

Clyde is currently living with a woman who works full-time. They built a house and split the bills. He gives his companion "a fair amount of financial assistance with her children." Getting them through college is the focus.

"It was kind of the deal when you sign on as a stepfather. You're either part of the team, or you're not."

The Counselor

Mike, who is on the verge of becoming an empty nester, said he has been wrestling the past few years with his own 50s crisis. Several years before he got married, he was in the military living in Europe while his male friends routinely traveled throughout the continent, having all sorts of escapades. He envied those friends.

Most of his married and child-rearing years have been dedicated to raising a family and spending money on the kids.

"And I'm about to end that," he said. "We've reached a time, when it would be great to focus more on ourselves. For (my wife) and I to travel more. Go back to doing a lot of the stuff I used to do, things like skiing, hiking, back packing."

Mike, 55, also talked about plans for an upcoming vacation he and his wife are taking to Hawaii, where the kids will join them afterward as well as an extended family reunion in Oregon.

"That's the beginning of trying to capitalize on doing something different. Celebrating our lives together," he said, noting college costs for the kids will end soon.

We talked about how he and his wife have managed their finances throughout the years, and who has called the shots. Mike's wife has a full-time job at a local university.

"How you use your money is so foundational to the choices you make and the lifestyle you live." In some cases, you may only have a chance to do something once. So the anxiety about how you choose to use it—what you say *yes* to, what you say *no* to—sometimes results in power struggles."

Throughout most of their marriage, "it's been mostly me, when she was home. In the traditional view of men carrying that angst... however, as women get involved in a dual career, they get involved (with the finances) as well," he said, adding that that is what has happened in his marriage.

Mike noted many marriages are "complementary," in that each person brings different approaches to things that end up complementing the relationship. That often is reflected in how couples handle their finances.

He and his wife, he said, are more "symmetrical," or similar.

"In money decisions, we tend to make similar decisions and our trouble is we both agreed to it. However, that creates problems elsewhere, because now we're going to have to pay for it, and we won't have that money at another time. We think we'll sacrifice later, but later isn't always that all thought out."

But the couple is also similar in that both often hesitate to spend money on themselves. He said they do not have separate checking or saving accounts designated for each other.

"When it comes to something I want for me... what usually happens is that the thought often disappears. I'll be thinking of other things and not in terms of me."

He said it is often his wife who encourages him to purchase new clothes, or to take a much-needed retreat by himself. He tries to do the same for her.

Afterthoughts

My wife has repeatedly said if I do not have anything to angst about I will find something. She is right. All through our marriage I have been the worry wart. Our finances have ranked right up there as being among my top concerns. Every big purchase, every vacation—it is always been me who has asked, *Are you sure we can afford this?*

At times, I have envied couples who pay for everything in cash. Laura on the other hand sees debt as a necessity of life—to get what we enjoy, what we need, what we deserve.

She is right. The purchase of our house, our cars, student loans, loans for needed house repairs—it is all necessary debt. And in hindsight, I would not trade the family vacations we have taken, or the trip to visit my daughter while she was a Rotary exchange student in Denmark.

Our current debt makes me feel uncomfortable, but we are paying it down. It has not caused any issues. However, I worry and continue to worry about it. That is just me. You never know. Things could change for us both—job-wise—on a moment's notice.

Like I said, as I came into middle age and got deeper and deeper into my shell, I was very conscious of the fact that we were spending less and less on ourselves (together) for fun. We were not going out on dates, and there was about a four-year stretch when we had no overnight getaways as a couple. I rationalized that one big reason this was happening was because we did not have the money.

Deep down I kept thinking, how could she be spending all this money on herself? It seemed to be snowballing, getting worse. That Annapolis trip brought out the worst of my fears.

Talking it out afterward during counseling, I finally looked at the hard numbers and realized Laura was not draining our bank account, or spending an ungodly amount of money on her recreational and girlfriend getaway pursuits.

Most importantly, we agreed to resume the overnight getaways (at least twice a year) and to start spending more money on us.

I also set up a separate banking account in which fifty dollars each week would be automatically deposited. Now, there would be no excuse not to spend money on myself—for a fishing trip, clothes purchase, whatever. If nothing else, I see it as a sort of separate savings account that we can tap on a moment's notice in a pinch—and on several occasions I have for such things as car repairs.

Finally, Laura assembled a comprehensive spread sheet of what we had coming in each week, and what was going out. It included a summary of our savings, our overall debt—along with a game plan for reducing it—and finally a wrap up of our retirement and insurance situations.

Does Laura still pay the bills? Yes. It has worked for nearly 30 years of our marriage and I am not about to mess with it. I know now where we stand—and get periodic updates—and that has made a big difference in our relationship.

But damn it, I still worry.

CHAPTER 10

OUR AGING BODIES

Forty is the old age of youth; fifty the youth of old age.
~ Victor Hugo, novelist, poet

Middle age is the time when a man is always thinking that in a week or two he will feel as good as ever.
~ Don Marquis, humorist, journalist, author

I distinctly remember a promise I made to myself when I was on the track team in college. It was that no matter what, I had always be in good enough shape to get up any morning and be able to run a nice, easy, five miles.

Well, that five miles shrunk to three miles during my thirties, and then to two miles during my early forties. And then *the injury* happened.

I was about 45 and playing indoor soccer, making a sprint for a ball on a fast break. It felt like someone hit my right knee with a hammer. I went down in a heap and looked in horror at my leg, noticing my knee cap was nearly halfway up the front of my thigh.

I had ripped my patella tendon, that thick band just below your knee cap that holds the knee cap to your upper shin. I went to the hospital that night and surgery followed the next morning. I was bed-ridden for four weeks, out of work for five.

It took nearly a year of physical therapy, bicycling and other exercises before I could even jog a nice easy lap around a high school track. Yes, I slowly came back, but ever since I have not been able to muster anything more than an easy three miles. Even that fell off as I got older because of foot problems.

All that—coupled with balding, a small beer gut and high blood pressure (I've been on medication for at least 10 years now)—made turning 50 a bummer. Steadily, my weight started creeping up. The time I spent exercising went down. My self-esteem followed.

Here I was getting into this state of mind where I was 51 going on 75. I was turning into a slug. Looking back, it is no surprise I was resentful of Laura playing indoor soccer and softball.

My competitive, athletic days were gone and I started cutting back when it came to fun activities with others outside my comfortable zone of work and family. And then along came another woman showing an interest in me. Although I did not take her up on it for reasons I have already covered, the experience made me look at myself and the possibilities for life and love in a new light.

This body still had something to offer. It just needed some attention and fine-tuning.

The Entertainment Manager

Middle age marks the passage between your peak years physically, but not necessarily mentally, Steve said. He has this theory about the genesis of so-called mid-life crises—specifically, that there is an organic reason behind what we men are going through emotionally.

"There's a lot of things we tend to forget: that we are a physical, as well as an intellectual being," the 55-year-old theater executive said. "There's still something inside of us, probably located within a physical space that represents the storage of our past history as an organism and it's sometimes competing with the modern overlay. It's one of the reasons we have a problem with middle age—there's a part of us saying, *Why aren't you dead yet?*"

Steve says "the primitive voice" inside cannot help, 'because (it's) never traveled this part of the journey in life before.'"

For example, menopause for women in the old days was probably a sign of impending death.

"So, the problem with mid-life crises for men (and women), which started arising centuries ago wasn't that it was a mid-life crisis. It was in fact an end-life crisis. Actually, these mid-life crises are very, very, new to human beings."

Steve said emotionally he went through middle age in his late 30s, when he started panicking about getting older "and all that stuff."

Because his field demands it, he has kept himself in good shape. He is not sure what emotional age he is at now, but readily acknowledges the physical deterioration process has started, although it has been delayed somewhat at this point.

"It's just the genetics in our family, we're long livers," he said. "I don't wear glasses yet, but it will come."

For many the physical deterioration happens at different levels.

"And I imagine it has to be hell when it all happens at once," he said. "And if it's your time when your wife or partner is going through menopause, I mean, wow, it has to be a triple bad thing."

Summing up his level of conditioning, Steve said his weight is "Okay," but he would like to be "a little tighter. I think I've lost flexibility. I think I'd rather be a 33 (pant size) than a 34, but I can kind of deal with it."

He grabs exercise when he can, usually about three times a week in the gym. He said he would like to do it five times.

"I'm a creature of habit. I go in cycles," he said, adding he could probably benefit from having a workout partner. He is a very competitive person, but he channels that into his work.

"As far as sports are concerned, I don't do anything that would risk any of my joints or back. I want to be active well into my 80s. I just watch other guys and think, *Did you guys take any anatomy classes? Once you blow your knee, it is fucking gone. No, I'm not playing racquetball, and you shouldn't either.* I'd put that in the category of stupid."

Steve said at his work he us constantly surrounded by dancers and other theater people. To a large extent, their bodies are their source of income.

"We're all very careful. We take glucosamine (a tendon and joint strengthening, dietary supplement), we stretch. Our bodies, even mine, for directing and choreography, it's very important that all my pieces work and I would never risk that on any of that (sports) stuff."

The Mechanic

Bob concedes he is wearing out, that he is not 25 anymore.

"I'm okay with that," the 47-year-old said. "I'm at about 75 percent," he added, describing his fitness level.

"Ideally, there's a lot of things I would like to do physically. I want to play soccer, go running up and down hills. Realistic? Probably not, but I still would like to do all that stuff."

Life continues to be busy and he has reached a point where competitive sports are no longer in the picture. He talked about how he recently blew his knee out.

"The doctor said I should have surgery, but here's a situation that shows the way I think. He tells me I'll be 16 weeks out of work. Okay, I can compromise right now. I'm not going to play sports. I don't have to have it done. So I work with it."

Bob prefers to stay active with a local scuba diving club, an activity he enjoys with his wife and children. He has a host of friends and acquaintances through the club.

Apart from that, he and his wife try to continue working out together. That happens, he said, but not as much as he would like.

"But my job is pretty physical. I stay in shape just doing that."

His greatest fear is "getting sick and having my whole life just crumble. You wonder how you would be if you got terminally ill, had leukemia, brain cancer, a week or a month to live. Or you get a massive stroke and end up being a paraplegic the rest of your life. That would suck," he said. "If something like that would happen, it would throw everything you've worked for your entire life right out the window."

The Police Officer

David, 48, was quick to respond when asked if he was happy with his level of conditioning and his health.

"No. Not particularly. As a matter of fact, I just hired a trainer. I need to drop a couple of pounds."

And for David, who weighs more than 250 pounds, it could be a matter of life or death. His "ideal weight" is about 200 to 205.

"My father, a brother and recently an uncle died in their 40s, early 50s. Heart disease. That's why I got my trainer, got on a diet, everything. It runs in my family. Particularly since I'm up around that age when they passed. I have to see what I can do about staying on this earth a little longer."

His greatest fear is dying before "I achieve what I want to achieve. And that's travel and growing older with my wife. We came together before our children, we raised our children and now I want to see what the other end looks like."

For years, David said, he used competitive sports to keep in shape.

"I'm very competitive. I played softball, touch football, basketball. Then I started regularly pulling muscles. That's why I picked up golf. I figured it would be a sport that I could continue to do."

He says golf is something he is very passionate about. He's in several leagues.

"It's like a sanctuary. When the weather breaks, you can find me out practicing or playing nearly every day."

The Counselor

Mike, 55, stressed the importance of talking care of one's self physically in middle age.

"Making it important, actually, is another thing," he said.

He feels the need to go back to playing sports, because simple exercise is boring.

"I have to come up with playing sports (on a team or something) that keeps me in there. But there's this time crunch. It's one of those things that went out the window."

Mike said there is a number of things he used to do before that he just cannot do now.

"You just get hurt easier."

For example, he was swimming laps on a regular basis. But it affected his neck (while doing the breast stroke).

"I have a bit of arthritis there. I did physical therapy to get out of that. You've heard the joke. *He still thinks he's 20.* There is some aspect to that. We don't want to adjust that our bodies are now different. But we need to be aware of that."

One big problem with middle-aged guys and sports, he said, is that men can simply be too competitive to their own detriment. It is a big difference between men and women in similar situations.

"If we don't have that relational connection, than I think what we're left with is competitiveness. When you go into sports, into those environments, the thing that balances competitiveness is the relationship connection. If there's not enough of that, the competitiveness gets out of control."

He cited the example playing soccer against a friend.

"There's a point where I'm not going to hurt you to score a goal, because I know you and I'm hanging out with you for other reasons."

Mike said many middle-aged men fail to seek that connection with those they are playing with, or competing against in team sports.

"They're getting together for the wrong reasons. For guys, we're too much interested in the task and the experience. Our emotional state gets very much into the competition. We're struggling with our own personal worth and value (in those situations). The relationships would help all those issues out."

Afterthoughts

About three years after I shredded my knee, I tried cycling and then light jogging to get myself back in shape. Then one spring weekend evening, following a light rain, my daughter, who was running outdoor track in high school at the time, suggested she and I go out for a run of about three miles.

For years, there was never a question about leading or keeping up with her. This time was different. We set off, and after about a quarter mile from the house, I stopped short in the road. Katie started off fast and was pulling away. I just could not keep up. I waved her on and walked dejectedly back to the house.

Other guys with children who I talked to had similar tales, of reaching a point where physically they were overtaken by their children. It is that competitive thing again. And take it from this competitive-as-hell guy, it hurts.

Vic, the middle school teacher who I mentioned earlier, told how his 12-year-old son was suddenly in better running shape than him. He also talked about a foul-shooting contest.

"I shot 9 out of 10, and this little shit stands up and shoots 10 out of 10. I never heard the end of it that night," he said. "You know… you see your skills deteriorating, but you fight it. I'm not going to admit that it's happening."

Some guys fight it harder than others.

Hugh, the divorced 50-year-old insurance man, admits he is a little overweight. He said he used to ski and play a lot of ice hockey, which he doesn't do anymore. He still plays softball and touch football, though he admits it may be his last year for the latter sport.

"A lot of people say I don't care about my body, that I'm reckless. When I skied I was doing flips, helicopters and going through barns. I broke my ankle twice in ski boots."

He continued being active with softball and touch football.

"I had my shoulder done twice, broke ribs, had concussions, broke fingers. I've woken up and gone to work with black eyes."

Is he and possibly many middle-aged guys too competitive for their own good, I asked?

"I think a lot of middle-aged guys should be doing more than what they do," he said. "A lot of them just shut themselves down."

Some do not. Call it good genes, a positive attitude, the incentive provided by younger children or a girlfriend or wife—whatever—they keep going. Two divorced guys I talked to said they were in the best shape of their lives, running, playing soccer.

However, the majority reflected the attitude of Tony, the attorney, who had been recovering for two years from emergency back surgery.

"I think of my body as the Acropolis," he said. "At one point, it was quite an impressive building. And now it is a decaying structure, although I'm working to fix that."

All this reinforced conversations I had beforehand with my surgeon and physical therapist during the rehab of my knee. They both told me if I wanted to continue staying active at my past levels I had to undergo intensive, additional physical therapy and conditioning—and to keep it up.

Otherwise, I had to come to terms with the fact that I needed to change my life and attitudes about sports, about doing physical things. No more soccer or basketball, I was told. Stick to jogging, cycling, tennis, walking—lower impact stuff.

For me, it was one of the major changes I went through in middle age. It came down to this: okay, your body and the fitness level that served you so well in the past will never be like it was when you were 20. Here is your new body for the second half of your life. Stop looking back, stop sulking and deal with it.

One other thing: Don't blow it. Continue being active, but at a slower clip. Take care of yourself.

I began following my doctor's advice and paying attention to my health. That meant watching my numbers—my weight, my blood pressure, my cholesterol figures. I have known several people recently who have suffered heart attacks and strokes in their late 40s and early 50s. It is not pretty.

I stopped putting salt on my food. Every morning, I pop a baby aspirin, a blood pressure pill and fish oil tablets. I try to work out several times each week at the gym at work. I play tennis. I am planning to get into cycling and swimming. I have been doing yoga.

Bottom line: taking care of your body through proper exercise and diet is a major, major part of staying active physically, mentally, and yes, sexually—in middle age and afterward.

I joke with my wife occasionally about whether we will still be *doing it* when we're 75 or 80.

"I hope so," she says.

CHAPTER 11

GETTING TOGETHER WITH THE GUYS

Friendship is a sheltering tree.
~ Samuel Taylor Coleridge, poet, literary critic, philosopher

Remember, no man is a failure who has friends.
~ From the movie, *It's a Wonderful Life*

In one scene from the 2009 movie, *It's Complicated*, actress Meryl Streep is a middle-aged woman lamenting her sex-less, post-divorce situation before a group of female friends over glasses of wine in a living room.

The conversation is hilarious, specifically as one woman's comments about how if an older woman stops having sex her vagina will simply close up, sealing itself permanently.

What stood out for me in this scene, though, was the group of females, who you get the sense meet together regularly for drinks. They are Streep's support group—life coaches if you will—as she negotiates the shoals of being single and unattached in middle age.

They epitomize what I have been saying all along. Many middle-aged women see the need and act upon it when it comes to carving out time in their lives for female friends. The book clubs, the weekly drinks at the local bar with the girls, the morning walks with best friends, and the all-girl getaways—they are all things that are marked on women's personal and family calendars and taken seriously.

And the middle-aged guys? Well, it is complicated. We often do not seem to get it, to understand the importance. The mantra of us married guys is that our wife is our best friend. Right?

I said it before and it is worth repeating. It is sad when your wife is your best and only friend and you are having marital problems.

Is this the genesis of many affairs or mid-life crises? I really don't know, but it certainly contributed to my situation, and I almost acted upon it by chasing after a woman I once dated.

So at age 51, I decided to start from ground zero. Rather than sit at home feeling sorry for myself because no one ever called me up to go fishing, or nobody ever called me up to go out for a beer, or that nobody ever called me up for anything—I took a new tactic.

The first step was taping the note card reading, *It won't happen unless I do it*, on my bathroom mirror.

I started off with the idea of a co-ed volleyball team. At least I would not be sitting home alone Thursday nights while my wife was out with her crew, I thought.

It was tough going at first. I kept getting the same reaction from friends.

"Let me get this straight," they'd say. "You're forming a co-ed volleyball team and your wife isn't playing?"

My answer was that I would include her if I could, but that she was already involved with her girlfriends doing indoor soccer. She was booked.

Bottom line: I formed the team and although some of the faces have changed and it's been like pulling teeth to get people to go out afterward to socialize, we have been together for about five years.

From there, I put together a low-stakes poker club that meets once a month.

I made it a point to resume going on an annual fishing trip with my brother-in-law and his friends. I also started a tradition of an annual getaway, camping weekend with another close friend in the Adirondacks each fall—around the same time my wife takes off with her buddies for their annual kayaking weekend.

I try to meet every Friday morning for breakfast with my close friend, David. And finally, as a result of interviewing guys for this book, I inspired one of the men to create a summer-time horseshoe throwing club that meets once a week and goes out for beers afterward.

Was it too much? For some, maybe.

But it has helped me regain that sense of balance in my life that I obviously needed. Resentment toward my wife and her outside activities quickly evaporated.

As I entered middle age, I finally got it. If I am not busy getting connected and staying connected, I am getting disconnected from some important things in life.

The Office Manager

Tracy, 52, has been trying to get his career back on track after being laid off from a company where he had worked for more than two decades.

"They called me in one Friday… and that was it, after all those years," he said.

He got a new job, but started from scratch with vacation, only getting two weeks.

Tracy does not like being called middle-aged.

"Middle age, it's a mindset. Like they said, the 60s are the new 40s. As long as we think like and feel like we're young, there's no middle age."

He talked of playing indoor soccer about eight years ago, before he blew his knee out.

"Oh, it was fun to start with, but it could be a little bit intense. I wanted to have fun, work on my ball skills. I really didn't care who won or lost. We had too many people get hurt, tempers flaring. That's not a comfortable situation. I don't need that in my life now."

Tracy readily conceded that his wife, who works full time at a local business, is more socially oriented than he. Now that his kids are in college, he said at times he feels lonely when his wife is away on business or with girlfriends.

"I clean the house, do my ironing, getting it done for the week. I'll sit back, read a book, and listen to some music. There's not a lot for me to do in town during the winter. I don't have a large group of friends like my wife has."

He and his wife belong to the local country club. Why not go there?

"I'd feel kind of guilty going over by myself to have a couple of drinks and a dinner by myself. It isn't my stuff," he said.

But during the summer months, he does have friends and activities that keep him busy. One is a tennis league in which games are held at private residences throughout the community. For years it was all men, but recently it has gone co-ed "to be politically correct," he said. Still, he likes the games, which allow him to keep in touch with friends and acquaintances in the community.

When asked if there were any activities with male friends that he would consider "sacrosanct," Tracy listed two.

One is the Sunday morning golf game during the summer with his father-in-law and two brothers-in-law at the local country club.

"The club has always known us as the family foursome. Many respect that. Think it's the greatest thing in the world. It's something we expect to do every year."

Another activity, however, is a notch above that—something that takes priority each year when it comes to using up his scant vacation time.

"I'm probably the happiest when I'm camping each spring in the Adirondacks with my best friend, Sean. And being with other friends from high school, and friends who come with them," he said. "We go up to the St. Regis Canoe Wilderness area (in the Adirondacks). I won't tell you where my sacred fishing holes are."

For months leading up to the trip, Tracy said he and Sean exchange phone calls and emails ironing out all the details. Tracy talked of waking up before the sun rises, having that first cup of coffee and sitting near a campfire. Feet up, relaxing, taking in the sunrise, listening to the sounds of the loons on the nearby lake.

"Sean and the guys call it a *Tracy morning.* It's when it's dead quiet. Foggy," he said. "I'll go out fishing by myself for at least two to three hours, and come back in. It's pure heaven. It's a special place."

The Financial Consultant

Mark, a financial consultant, said he is certainly not at the extreme end of being introverted, "but I'm probably with those leanings."

He talked of working long, hard hours during the week—a grind that he has been on for years now.

The 50-year-old said he celebrated his 50th birthday with little fanfare.

"I just think we had dinner. I really don't like parties of that kind, so it was really, by intention, low-key. Maybe there was a cake. And that's all there was."

I asked him about loneliness.

"Well, I'm not often alone. It's not like I'm in the house for extended periods of time, alone."

He said when his wife is gone for extended periods of time, though, such as weekend, he gets a sense of what it would be like.

"It would be hard. I'm not sure what I would do."

Mark notices the difference between himself and his wife when it comes to needing or wanting friends.

"That's something that's apparent between women and men. My wife needs to have her friends. I think it's nice, enjoyable, but I don't know if there's a compulsory need. I see her talking. I see this need that she needs to talk to somebody. I don't know if I necessarily feel that need."

I asked him if there was anyone he would feel comfortable calling in the case of an emergency, say if he was stuck at the airport on a late Sunday evening and could not reach a family member for a ride.

"I don't know that I can necessarily say that I have a best friend, somebody who's a right-hand person who's always there," he said, though adding he does have a couple of friends he would consider calling.

He "sort of enjoys" seeing those two friends occasionally. "And there's guys that I hang out with at work. I also have a new neighbor about two doors down. We run three days a week together."

He emphasized he is not a team sports player, but conceded when it comes to running and working out, "it's a helluva lot easier to get up at 5 a.m. when it's four degrees out and blowing like hell when you know someone else is showing up at the door."

He said he has never been involved in any kind of annual, sacrosanct, all-male getaway of any sort. "When we first moved here, we were very, very busy with work and the house. That can be an excuse. I just feel if I'm going to do anything, I'd just as soon go camping with my family."

He said even after his son has gone to school, there was nothing he thinks about doing with other guys—though he did mention a neighbor who gets away with high school buddies once or twice a year camping "or something like that." It is a closed group. They often bring their sons.

"It used to be when they were in high school, they'd see how much beer they could drink… and he jokes about it," he said. "It's a lot slower now. It might be kind of nice, but I just don't feel the need."

He emphasized that over the years his work has taken, and continues to take, a lot of his time—leaving little for such things as coaching youth teams or any kind of community service.

I asked him if it was necessary for him to occasionally do something "selfish," to find something outside of his work and family that's "self-nurturing."

"Nothing comes to mind. I don't necessarily say I agree with that statement," he said.

However, the one thing he has found time for lately is blacksmithing. He took a class and learned the basics. He has since set up an anvil and a forge in his garage.

"It's incredible to work with, and move metal as if it's a plastic material. The world of it is huge. Everything from very functional, utilization items such as hooks and fire pokers, to very artistic things. I see myself doing more of the things you'll use on a day-to-day basis. For Christmas, I made some heart-shaped trivets for people."

But during much of the winter months, he puts this equipment away. His garage is unheated. "It's too stinking cold," he said. Regardless, "I see doing more of that."

The Carpenter

Frank's job as a carpenter is demanding physically, and he strives to keep in shape. Being single, 54, and out on the dating scene, he is determined not to let his body go. His group of guy friends helps.

"At my age, it takes a lot more tuning. You can't get away with neglecting yourself as much," he said. "Over-eating, not exercising, over-drinking. The decline quickly starts. Like you can run for years and take off two months and you lose a lot of fitness. It's tricky at my age, but it's there."

Frank said he needs help, motivation to continue to work out. That comes from a group of guys he gets together with at least once a week to run.

It has paid off.

"Lately, I did a 10-mile race, keeping a 7-minute pace. It's there, but I need help and I draw from anywhere I can… my buddies, my running partners."

He said men in general have this "fear of failing" thing in whatever they do.

"We're competitive. So we try to do heroic things, like a marathon, and then we tell everyone about it afterward."

Last year, he saw this 81-year-old guy finish a 10K race.

"So, I think about it. It's going to be there for me. But what do I need to do to make sure I keep in shape?"

Getting together regularly with the guys to work out has been, and will continue to be, a crucial element, he said.

Afterthoughts

While I have harped in this book about many guys being lonely or not taking time for male friendships, there are also guys out there on the other end of the continuum.

I am talking about guys who selfishly golf, fish, hunt—or whatever with their buddies—during all, or most of their free time.

These are guys who have lost or are losing the passion for their marriage. Guys who for selfish reasons are missing out on the joys of fatherhood by not spending enough time with their kids (and that is time they will never get back). Guys who should not be surprised when their wife announces "this isn't working" and walks out the door.

Their lives are out of balance in another way.

John, a caribou hunting guide who works in the wilds of British Columbia in Canada, told me I would not believe the number of married guys who during their hunts with him talk about having to make up for taking time and money spent on their outings by doing special things with, and for their wives upon their return.

That sounds fair to me.

But that was not me—far from it. And I am not alone. From all I have read, the past two decades have seen a decline in middle-aged guys participating in recreational groups, clubs and church. We are joining less, getting together less, having less fun with life.

I have said repeatedly much of the problem falls back on the shoulders of the guys themselves to do something about it. But there is a hesitation.

One thing I have noticed is this mentality that seems to be a creation of the baby-boomer generation. For many couples, their lives are completely centered on the kids. I am talking about the need to schedule their children's time each and every day and be somehow involved in many, if not all facets of their kids' lives—often to their own detriment.

Talk to the parents whose children are on traveling hockey, lacrosse or soccer clubs, the stage parents and on and on. Often, these parents are not involved in service clubs, church or recreational sports teams themselves—Overnight getaways with just each other or sacrosanct time away with friends are non-existent.

They will tell you about entire winters, summers and vacations dedicated to their kids' activities. They will tell you how they make every single game and scrimmage without fail and everything else falls by the wayside. It is a badge of pride. They are being ideal parents.

Don't get me wrong. I would be the last person, having coached youth sports and been active in other activities with my kids, to discourage parents from spending time with their children. I am talking, though, about those who go overboard, leaving nothing for themselves. In most cases, that cannot be good.

In addition, I have sensed that not all women buy into the idea that their husbands need time apart from their families with friends.

That is probably unfair, though, and I am not seeing the whole picture. Maybe the guys are just too busy with other aspects of their life. I have also chalked it up to the effects of those couples being in the child-rearing phase of their relationship, and the resulting "child care wars."

Women, particularly when the kids are young, often get dumped on big time in terms of dedicating time to the children. Guys need to recognize that and make a concerted effort to remedy that imbalance.

As the kids get older, the pressure and the spotlight is often turned more and more on Dad to spend time with them, by getting involved in such activities as coaching athletics, Boy Scouts and taking them fishing. I experienced this and many of my male friends have as well.

When I was going through that, I found slicing off time for myself and friends very difficult. I made the mistake of just forgetting about it or not wanting to bother.

However, social loneliness can be a downer. I don't care if you are an introvert or extrovert. It is the rare dude who does not need at least one friend, one person who he can call on in a pinch or in a moment of trouble or about a big problem.

Recently, a friend called me about going over to a local businessman's house to help him with his hot tub. He was working on repairing his heavy hot tub and had turned it up on its side to make a repair. However, he needed to move it, and he and his wife hesitated to do it themselves.

So there it sat for about half a week. Despite the fact that the guy served hundreds of customers locally, he did not feel he had anybody he could call to come over and help him move his hot tub.

The only way my friend found out about the local businessman's situation was that he had called him on an unrelated matter and got to talking about other things.

I went over and helped out, but I came away thinking this guy did not feel comfortable reaching out to anyone to help out. It was strange, but not uncommon. Four years ago I was exactly where he was.

When I first got actively involved in expanding my friendship base, I found the hardest part was reaching out and committing to time with friends. I had gotten into bad habits. I decided to take what I considered to be radical steps.

When a friend's father or mother died, I used to just send a card or do nothing at all. I began calling, or if I saw them out in public, stopping them and offering my personal condolences.

Whenever I heard of an acquaintance needing to move something, I offered and several times used or allowed them to use my truck to help out.

When someone I wanted to strengthen my friendship with mentioned wanting to go fishing, or do something else, I made it a point of following through and making it happen.

In time, they started calling me—offering congratulations, condolences or offering to help out with home, car or boat repairs. And they've called me to go fishing. This stuff builds on itself.

It all came down to committing, making it a priority.

As I have already said, there is no greater indication of a guy's ability to do that, or not, than the family calendar. That is the calendar that hangs on or near the fridge in many couple's homes.

I cannot tell you the number of times the guys in the activities I am involved in agreed to things, only to cancel out at the last minute because their wives alerted them they had something else scheduled, or some activity involving their kids that they forgot.

For too many years, I depended on Laura to run my social calendar. I know I am not alone.

My point is this: imagine trying to schedule a dinner at your house with another couple on the same night your wife has her monthly book club meeting, when she plays Bunco, plays softball, or on the night that she goes out faithfully with the ladies for a drink.

Nine times out of ten, it is not going to happen.

The top guy in our horseshoe throwing group (we call him "The Commissioner") has had to deal repeatedly with members who beg out at the last minute because of some personal conflict that their wife made them aware of, or who just no-show because they forgot.

His solution? Group members are required to email or call him (or the group's sergeant at arms) beforehand if they are not planning to show, and to explain briefly why. Failure to do so or citing some lame excuse has consequences. The violators are fined pitchers of beer, payable upon the next time they show at horseshoes.

The fines are listed in a weekly email newsletter The Commissioner (or his designee) sends out, recapping that week's throw and the highlights of the evening.

It is effective. Most of the guys are learning, marking the horseshoe group outings on their personal or family calendars. For those who do not and keep forgetting, it is a reminder of their lack of commitment, the lack of balance in their lives. Or, maybe it is the fact that they have over-extended themselves by being in our group in the first place.

Like I said, it is complicated. However, it is not insurmountable.

Feel the need for male companionship outside your marriage? My advice is to start small. Ask someone from work, or a parent you have met through your kids, out to breakfast, lunch or a drink.

Meanwhile, make a list of your interests and passions. Use the Internet to see what local groups exist. Put the word out and commit time to seek and reach out to like-minded individuals or groups—and follow through.

The options are endless. There are running and biking groups, birding, kayaking, fishing, rod and gun clubs, softball teams, pool and dart leagues, beer and wine making clubs, book clubs, bowling leagues, wildlife photography clubs, coin and stamp collecting groups—you name it.

If you are so inclined, start something from scratch. If you are uncomfortable doing it, or run into problems, don't be afraid to ask your wife or girlfriend for help. I know it may sound funny coming from a guy with years of management experience at newspapers, but more than once I found myself asking Laura, "Now, how would the women do this?"

I learned from Laura the importance of setting a date for an activity (the poker club, fishing trips, etc.), and sticking to it, and of putting it on the family calendar. She also showed me the effectiveness of email and text messaging (as opposed to constantly calling everyone) to communicate things. Most important, she advised me not to take rejection personally. "People have a lot of other things going on," she said.

One last thing: The idea that someone is going to call you out of the clear blue and invite you to join their group or activity is wishful thinking. More often than not, you have to make the first move.

CHAPTER 12

THE BOGEYMAN

Every man, through fear, mugs his aspirations a dozen times a day.
~ Brendan Francis, poet, short story writer, novelist and playwright

I have learned over the years that when one's mind is made up, this diminishes fear; knowing what must be done does away with fear.
~ Rosa Parks, African American civil rights activist who refused, when ordered, to move to the back of the bus

Fear is a relative thing.

For many guys I interviewed, their greatest fear is their premature death or the death of a family member—or the possibility of suddenly coming down with a debilitating sickness or injury following an accident.

It can also be a relationship thing—something to do with their wife, their girlfriend, or their kids.

One thing is for sure: having passed life's halfway mark, many men at this stage of life are taking stock of what they have, what makes them happy and what they stand to lose if life takes a horrible turn. Among the greatest fears mentioned:

> Death. You never can put a date on it. You can walk outside your door today and get run over. There's a lot of things I'd like to do (in life). The only thing I think about is how it's going to be.
> ~ Hugh, 50, insurance man, divorced

Cancer's the bogeyman. I have younger friends who died of cancer. I hope I can stay healthy. Cancer will kick the shit out of anyone. I don't care who you are.
~ Ian, 49, web page designer, divorced

I think it would be health-related, if something bad would happen to a family member. I could accept my own (death) because of my age. But if something happened to one of my kids—that's my greatest fear.
~ Al, 55, painting contractor, married

Dying before I achieve what I want to achieve—traveling and growing old with my wife. We've raised our children. Now I want to see what the other end (of life) is like.
~ David, 47, police officer, married

Failing my children. Missing opportunities (to be and do things with them) while they're still young.
~ Frank, 54, carpenter, divorced

My greatest fear is being lonely. I know what it's like to have a good relationship, to have a good companion. That's the reason I miss (my wife) so much.
~ Jeremy, 52, retail manager, widowed

I do a lot. I have students that look to me for learning and face-time. I have manuscripts I have to review. I do consulting work for oil and gas companies, often in third world countries. Each day I think about all this and at times it eats away at me. *Am I doing the right thing every day?* I often wonder.
~ Ivan, 54, college professor, married

> My greatest fear is doing (my) job for another 10 years, and not developing skills to do something else, not knowing what I would try. Who wants a 60 year old these days? Companies are making so many changes. There's the Internet and that's changed things. I know a guy who got laid off and he's now delivering groceries for $12 an hour, and another guy who can't get a job.
> ~ Rick, 61, sales, married

> I would like to reevaluate myself and reach for that next level of growth. My greatest fear is that I'd shirk from opportunities—from moving, or (going on) some mission for spirituality… it could be a new business venture. And frankly, I'm not completely happy with what I'm doing now. I probably only have a decade left before I retire. I don't want to play it safe, get too conservative. Why stop now and not take advantage of such an opportunity? That's my biggest fear.
> ~ Mike, 55, counselor, married

Afterthoughts

I was at a recent funeral of a friend's father. As I walked in the church looking for a familiar face, I spotted an old high school chum.

After a firm handshake and hug and wondering out loud why the hell "so and so" was not there, he said something that is so true in middle age.

"I guess we've just reached that age when people we know—parents in particular—start dying. This is the third funeral I've been to the past couple of weeks."

We guys can deny a lot of things, including the fact that our life is half over. But reality is a bitch. And a major part of that reality is that at our age we are the parents, the persons in charge.

In most cases, we are at the height or approaching the height of our careers and earning power. We are the ones being called to organize the family picnics and other family events, to make key decisions about our lives and those of our kids, about retirement, about caring for our ailing, aging parents.

But it is also the time of life when things start getting taken away. Age is affecting our health, our bodies. The presence of death in our lives becomes more pronounced as our parents, our friends' parents and others begin dying.

I initially thought this greatest fear question was a no-brainer. It's your death, the death of your children, cancer, getting paralyzed from the neck down. Things like that.

Not always. Some of the responses I got from guys prompted a lot of introspection on my part and actually contributed heavily to my decision to change my career path as a newspaperman.

With all that has been going on in the newspaper industry lately, one of my greatest fears has been getting laid off, or worse, coming to work one day and being told the newspaper is closing. That's been my bogeyman (and continues to be).

When I started this book I was working as a regional editor covering a city and a county for more than 15 years. There was a series of buyouts going on and a lot of change was in the air as staff shrunk, bureaus closed, sections were cut or eliminated and the overall size of the paper decreased.

I was hunkered down in my bureau, hoping I could keep plucking that same string, making that same sound—and hoping I could continue doing it right through retirement (some 10 years away). I was fooling myself.

Then the newspaper's outdoors writer announced his retirement. He was taking a buyout after some 20 years on the job. News of his retirement quickly spread.

I once told an upper level manager during an annual review that if I could have any other job in the newsroom it would be the outdoors writer. However, I joked at the time that the only way I would ever get it was if he was carried out of the newsroom in a coffin. I had no doubt he was solid in that job for life.

Well? Was I interested now? I inquired and was told I would be able to keep my editor's salary but my raises would dry up.

Initially, I said no. Despite being an undeniable "fishing nut" and loving the possibilities of covering the outdoors after years on the city desk, I worried about the security of the job.

Laura initially discouraged me, saying I was dropping out of what I do best (hard news) and going to a fringe area of the paper—that I was "putting myself out to pasture" and making myself an easy target if layoffs came.

Then I remembered my interview with Mike, the counselor, about his greatest fear being that an opportunity would come along to change his job, his career path, and that he wouldn't have the guts to make the move.

And one of the newspaper's editors confronted me in an aisle at the paper, amazed at my hesitation.

"Are you crazy? They're not going to cut your salary if you take the job," he said. "And what would you rather be doing from now until retirement? Sitting in a bureau covering school board elections and city council meetings, or writing about hunting and fishing?"

He said the decision seemed so clear, particularly since he himself had applied for the job.

I went home that night, put all the pros and cons on a legal pad and convinced myself and Laura that I should go for the job. I also drafted a proposal to significantly expand the coverage of the beat way beyond the traditional "hook and bullet" (hunting and fishing) stuff.

"I will cover everything from birding to bear hunting," I pledged during my interview, in addition to significantly expanding the Internet presence of the newspaper's outdoor coverage on my blog. The idea was to draw increased numbers of younger readers and women to the newspaper's sports pages and on-line report on Syracuse.com.

Several years have passed. I am talking about some of the happiest, most challenging, most rewarding years of my nearly 30-year newspaper career. I am trying out many things for the first time (hunting, birding, ice fishing) and writing about them with the passion of a wide-eyed newcomer. I have been told by many that my enthusiasm shows in my writing.

To help out, I have assembled a list of more than 1,600 readers from nearly every interest area in the outdoors. Each week I email them a report of what I am working on, what sources I need, etc. I also use Twitter, Google-Plus and have an Outdoors group on Facebook to keep in touch with sources and provide links to my stories online.

Don't get me wrong. I am working my tail off. And nearly seven days a week I am shoveling stuff into my Outdoors blog for the newspaper, keeping it fresh and readable.

More often than not, I am at my desk at the newspaper writing or working from home. However, I also have a great freedom to pick and choose what to work on.

I recently went pheasant hunting for the first time and shot my first pheasant. Same goes for wild turkey hunting.

Ever been out to check a trapping line? Gone mushroom picking with an expert and eaten what you found for lunch? Seen someone scale a 150-foot-high sheet of ice in a river gorge during the dead of winter? I have.

I collaborated with the golf writer on a story about fishing golf course ponds. We hit several links in golf carts, with tackle boxes and our poles sticking out the back. The golfers passing by couldn't believe their eyes.

When I hooked a 22-inch largemouth bass on a plastic worm in front of a par-three green, I waded into the pond up to my thighs to get past a mat of weeds that rimmed the edge. I did not have a net and I did not want to lose the fish.

When I grabbed it by the lower lip and held him up to the sky, I could not believe how fat he was and how hard he fought. He had jumped four times.

Do you believe this? I'm at work!

Lesson learned—again. It never would have happened during my middle age years if I did not make it happen.

CHAPTER 13

GUYS AND GOD

The old believe everything, the middle-aged suspect everything, the young know nothing.
~ Oscar Wilde, writer, poet and playwright

The long, dull, monotonous years of middle-age prosperity or middle-age adversity are excellent campaigning weather for the devil.
~ C.S. Lewis, novelist, poet, lay theologian

Is there a God for middle-aged men?

While a number of men I interviewed mentioned the importance of their faith, others were down on church and organized religion.

A Pew Research Center's Forum on Religion and Public Life survey in 2102 concluded the number of Americans who do not identify with any religion continues to grow at "a rapid pace." One fifth of those polled—and a third under the age of 30—are religiously unaffiliated.

The Pew survey, conducted jointly with the PBS television program, *Religion and Ethics NewsWeekly*, found two thirds (68 percent) expressed a belief in God, more than half (58 percent) felt a strong connection with nature and the earth (58 percent) and a third (37 percent) described themselves as being "spiritual" but not "religious." [13]

The older one gets, the more likely an individual is to claim a religious affiliation. Women outnumber men in voicing affiliation during middle age, the survey found.

Pew found that even among the unaffiliated, most feel that churches and other religious institutions strengthen community bonds and help the poor. However, strong feelings were also expressed that they are too concerned with "money and power, too focused on rules and too involved in politics."

I live in Skaneateles, N.Y., a small village in Central New York that frankly is as white-bread as they come. We have a miniscule number of minorities. There are no ethnic parts of town—no Italian, Polish, Irish sections, for example, which you will find in many older cities.

Our churches are essentially Catholic, mainstream Protestant (Lutheran, Episcopalian, Methodist, Presbyterian, Baptist) and one non-denominational, Bible-oriented, evangelical church that appears to be the fastest growing of the lot.

When I started taking a hard look at what I was going through in middle age, my church and the other men in it weren't much help. The reasons?

I did not think to look there. There was no involvement, no commitment on my part. There were men actively involved in church activities, but no men's group. There had not been one for 15 years. There was no one who I regularly socialized with outside of Sunday worship, despite being a member for more than five years.

We had a female minister. It seemed women were often playing the dominant role in church activities and deciding matters of worship, even what music was used. I saw a lot of women attending church without their husbands. It is something I have since learned is not unique to our church. [14]

Looking back, the role and importance of faith in my life has waxed and waned. As a college student, I considered becoming a Roman Catholic priest. I had short stints in a Campus Crusade for Christ group and briefly attended a Bible study. Afterward, I began attending noontime Mass at the Cornell University chapel one to two times during the week, in addition to Sunday services.

However, my mother's sickness and premature death at 51 from breast cancer rocked my faith to its roots, rotting them.

After she died I simply stopped going to church. I rarely, if ever prayed. For years, I would tear up (and still do at times) when I think about Mom, who never got to know my wife and never got to see and love her grandchildren.

Some 15 years later, though, I stopped into a small, rural Catholic Church on the way home from an afternoon of trout fishing in the Catskills. I was drawn by the sign out front: *Confessions, 4:30 p.m.*

I took off my hip boots and went in. After earnestly praying for about 15 minutes, I went inside the confessional. I was shocked when the priest refused to hear my confession, chastising me for living in sin the past 15 years after I told him my wife and I were married by a justice of the peace, rather than by a Roman Catholic priest.

He told me we would have to take a several-month-long marriage preparation course and then get officially married in the church before he would hear my confession.

I could not believe what I was hearing and I told the priest as much. I walked out of the church in a huff. I came home all worked up and angrily told my wife what had happened.

I also told friends and they recommended another Catholic Church in a nearby town. We attended it and the priest there heard my confession several weeks later, no questions asked.

But the damage was done. I know I cannot judge all Catholic priests on the actions of one, but I could not get it out of my head. My beef was not with God, it was with the church.

That confession incident, and the Catholic Church's later bungling and revelations of the church's inexcusable denials for years on the whole child-molesting priest thing eventually contributed to me turning my back on my Roman Catholic upbringing.

Today, I belong to a Methodist church. My faith in God at times varies from intense to tepid, depending on what is happening in my life and with my family. I often find myself trying to intellectualize God's existence.

I began attending church regularly for three reasons:

I felt the need to be there for my kids, to give them a sound, moral compass and hopefully to feel the presence of God in their lives.

I yearned for a strong sense of community, something I had been lacking for years as a journalist who prided himself in never joining anything and remaining objective, separate from the crowd.

I had a strong need, a desire to give thanks to God for what I have. And also, for help in directing and conducting my life.

Having worked in newspapers for years, I have written and edited stories about how someone's world can turn upside down following one accident, one illness or one fateful mistake. Life is so damn fragile.

I know I am lucky. I have a great wife, a great job and great kids. We all are in good health. No one's in jail. My wife and children are not hooked on drugs or alcohol.

There, but for the grace of God go I, has popped into my mind more times than I care to remember. It is especially at those times that I feel the need to humbly and appreciably thank God for what I have. A sampling of comments from other men follow:

God doesn't have to see you in his house to know if you're living by the basic 10 rules or not. That's the way I look at it. I haven't been to church in years.
But I did have an experience back in college, while playing indoor soccer. I went way up for a scissors kick (some 36-38 inches) and came right down on my neck. I remember hearing the smash. I thought I was dead on the spot. I was out for about a half hour. I had more people say afterward, 'We're surprised you're not dead, let alone a paraplegic.' Was there some kind of intervention? I was very, very fortunate and I've always believed (there was something apart from me, and bigger than me that happened that day). Do I pray? Now, maybe after a sporting event, whatever… or if I want to say hello to someone, such as my wife's mom who passed away 12 years ago.
~ Tracy, 52, office manager, married

I'm very religious and it's the center of our family. We've made sure that we've raised our children to be respectful, to have a certain sense of spirit, or spirituality to them. It's because you have to have faith in something. You have to believe in a higher being. I was brought up in the church, but I haven't been back to church in a while. I just feel we (should) live the way God would want us to live. Do I pray? Every day on the way to work.
~ David, 48, police officer, married

I'm what you'd call spiritual. I'm not religious. Sitting in church, my mind starts to wander. It's just doesn't do it for me. But anytime I'm out in nature, say at the end of the pier looking out into the lake during the early morning, it makes me think there had to be intelligent design behind all that. Nature makes me believe in God.

~ Rick, 61, sales, married

I go to Mass every Sunday, but I'm pretty shaky on a lot of it. I have huge problems obviously with the church and religion in general. This whole anti-science stuff. But, it's just been part of me. I was an altar boy. My mother was very devout. I'm one of those guys, when things go bad, I'm right there. The more you read… the lives of popes, the whole thing, the more you delve into it… it's on very thin ice. Now there is some higher power someplace. I'm like Jefferson. A deist. But I do participate. I'm a lay minister and all that stuff. Sometimes I feel a little hypocritical about it all. But so much of life has evolved socially around the church through the years, especially when we didn't have any money. For the youth… dances, youth parties, Boy Scouts. It was the center of my social life for a long time.
~ Scott, 60, retired teacher, married

My faith is central. It's a primary value in my life. It's an organizing world view. Yet at the same time, during this part of my life, it's part of a re-evaluation. I'm hoping that the questions, the disappointments and discussions that I'm having, where I'm willing to look at contradictions and concerns in areas of fulfillment—that all this will push me to a more mature, spiritual point of view. I go to church and try to live more conscientiously because I either want to be there for me or the family, or because I want to go and give. My field is counseling, and I look at that as a ministry—my ministry. I'm conscientious about giving in that area. I've taught on certain subjects and been involved in men's groups, or marital sessions. I'm also involved with a group call the Navigators… where we're trying to bring together groups of men

who would be looking at their application of faith as they work. So there's a lot of social networks.
~ Mike, 55, counselor, married

I'm not a particularly religious person and do not routinely attend church. I don't belong to any. But I think I very strongly adhere to what I would consider the basic elements of religion. If everyone lived by the Ten Commandments, we wouldn't have any problems. There are some very basic elements of consideration and respect, and if everyone abided by them, most of the human conflict would be gone. There are just numerous people who attend church religiously on Sunday and would cut your throat on Monday morning and not give it a second thought… and sleep with your wife after the church service if they could get away with it. They don't really mean the things they say. I much prefer somebody to mean what they say, and don't say it if you don't mean it.
~ Frank, 54, carpenter, divorced

I often think about going back to church. I'm not sure when. I used to go when I was younger. I'm spiritual, but I don't practice. It's funny, my father, who's 77, has been going to church for a number of years now. I think it's an inner peace thing. It's never too late. You can always do it (proclaim your faith to God) in the last few seconds of your life. But I feel healthy. I'll be around for a while. In the latter part of life, it's cleaning up loose ends. Like cleaning up the attic. Getting rid of the clutter.
~ Sky, 51, pilot

Afterthoughts

So, why wasn't there a men's group at my church?

I delved a little into it, but I could not get a clear answer. Several men I talked to mentioned a time when families in the church were a lot closer. They mentioned a church-initiated dinner club that brought many couples together at each other's homes. The dinner club thing ended more than a decade ago, they said.

I discussed this with my dentist, with whom I had been talking about this book on middle-aged men I was working on. He was involved in medical-related mission work and I was impressed by his passion for what he was doing. He invited me to his church (one of the other mainstream Protestant churches in the village) to attend a meeting of a newly formed men's group there.

Interested in what was going on, I decided to check it out. The group started out with nearly a dozen, mostly middle-aged guys. The discussion (after we exchanged personal stories) centering on a purely spiritual emphasis, including attending an upcoming retreat designed for men. Several months passed. The last meeting of the group was a bust. The only two there were the group leader and I.

In their book, *The Leading Causes of Life*, authors Gary Gunderson and Larry Pray noted, "The (church) congregations that open themselves to the real needs of people stop talking at them and start talking with them—coming along beside them, becoming involved in their lives." [15]

Why did this one particular group effort at my dentist's church sputter? Probably for several reasons. I really did not know any of these guys very well. It could have been a matter of timing, or personalities. My thoughts were that the group leader was talking at us, and simply not supplying something that the men really wanted or felt they needed. End of story.

I returned to my church and mentioned the need for a men's group. Three guys, who were long-term members, expressed interest. We met for breakfast and came up with three areas to focus on: spiritual, social and service in the community.

The guys asked me to be the keynote speaker at the group's first breakfast meeting to talk about what I had discovered while researching for this book. I agreed.

At Sunday's service the week before, one of the guys, Steve, announced the upcoming breakfast meeting to the congregation. He made a point of saying, "And this is not your father's men's group."

I used that phrase in my speech the following week at the breakfast, explaining I personally felt the need for the exact opposite of what Steve was implying. I wished deep down that it would become like my father's men's group.

Dad grew up in Binghamton, N.Y. He went to a church mostly attended by Ukrainian and other Eastern European immigrants. From an early age, he and his buddies played softball, bowled and partied. And they belonged to The Omega Club, a Catholic Church-based social group.

Almost all were in the service during World War II and when they came back they returned to their faith and their social ties in the Omega Club. This club stuck together for years, not only being involved in church activities, but engaging in social events that were always on our family calendar—picnics, Christmas and other holiday get-togethers, dances, clam bakes and horseshoe tournaments.

I grew up going to the weddings of many of the Omega Club member's children.

Bottom line: these men had a major influence on my father's life. I always got the feeling that any one of these guys would have been there for him, or our family in a moment of need.

Here in Skaneateles, N.Y., it is no surprise (at least to me) that the one church in our community that is rapidly growing in size (the evangelical one) has a host of male-only groups and activities—including a wild game dinner each year that draws a packed house of guys of members and non-members. I am sure that is not the only reason the church is growing, but it is worth noting.

At our group's first breakfast, I talked about the need to address all areas of our mission statement, particularly the social part, if we were ever to get in gear.

My point was that guys in our congregation, if they chose to join the group, would come together at various different stages and levels of faith and that a number of activities could be offered to address that. Also, our goal of serving others could be satisfied by organizing and scheduling events or programs.

The most difficult part, though, would be the creation and nourishment of relationships between us. That would only take place as a result of doing things that true friends do—having fun through a variety of experiences, sharing personal thoughts (including, joys, sadness, and problems) and committing to each other.

I am talking about getting to the point where we would invite each other over for dinner, attend each other's parties, funerals, weddings, graduation parties—possibly hunt, fish together. Form a book club. Maybe go out for a beer or pizza together on the spur of the moment.

The men's group at my church has taken hold, but the momentum waxes and wanes. Members have participated in a number of activities and projects. We averaged about four to six breakfasts a year, often with guest speakers. However, it still has a long ways to go. The social aspect of the group outside of church is still lacking.

I have raised the issue and tried to take a leadership role. However, my commitment at times, I am sad to say, has not been as strong as it should be. I have struggled with that. I am just as guilty as the next guy for not being involved, for not walking the walk.

The Rev. Rick Warren, in his book, *The Purpose Driven Life*, notes that the most vibrant churches are those whose members not only pray together and worship together, but who develop close friendships, share experiences and give support to each other.

"Real fellowship happens when people get honest about who they are and what is happening in their lives," he said.[16]

Bottom line: keeping the momentum going by connecting and staying connected with each other is what a full life—a life of happiness, of satisfaction, of having one's needs met—is all about.

That holds true whether you go to church or not.

CHAPTER 14

GUYS WHO GET IT

Friendship is born at that moment when one man says to another: 'What! You too? I thought that no one but myself…
~ C.S. Lewis, novelist, poet, lay theologian

Friendship needs no words—it is solitude delivered from the anguish of loneliness.
~ Dag Hammarskajold, diplomat, economist, author

One of the joys of doing this book was talking with men about the fun, supportive and rejuvenating times they have had, and continue to have with other guys.

They inspired me.

For some, it is an annual getaway. For others, it is more frequent get-togethers. Some men quoted below are middle-aged. Others are older, retired. Either way, their stories and their comments were refreshing to hear.

The 'Once-in-a-Lifetime' Fishing Trip

Bill, a retired engineer in his early 70s, said that during his working years he held a stressful, high-powered job at a local firm. Just after he turned 40, he began talking up the idea of a fishing getaway with his buddies.

"We would say to each other, 'We ought to go on one of those Canadian fishing trips,'" he said. "This went on and on. We called it our once-in-a-lifetime trip. Finally, we just said, 'We're going to do it.'"

Bill said he noticed an ad in the back of a fishing magazine, made the call, and in 1979 convinced three friends to take a week-long trip to Opichawan Lake in a desolate northern region of Ontario Province.

He remembers the morning they left. One of his friends had just been made a partner in the engineering firm where Bill worked and he had bought a new station wagon—the vehicle they were planning to use on the trip. Rushing around, the friend accidentally dented the back of his new vehicle.

The guys were undaunted. "We just said, 'Heck, we're going fishing' and left," Bill said.

The foursome drove 1,000 miles northward to a Canadian airport. They then flew more than 150 miles into the lake in a vintage, 1942 float plane.

They stayed a week. Bill remembers the accommodations being "crude." They all stayed in tents and used an outhouse. The bugs were thick at times. They brought their own food, but also used the fish they caught as their main course at dinners each night.

"We just had so much fun," he said.

At the end of the week, the float plane returned with the next group of guys—guys who were in their 50s and 60s.

"We looked at these guys and vowed right there and then we were going to keep going every year we possibly could."

Since that first year, the group has taken off a week each summer for more than 30 years, fishing 15 Canadian lakes. One guy dropped out, but others, including Bill's brother and all the other men's sons and nephews, have come along at one time or another.

Bill said he and his buddies have talked numerous times "about this trip being one of the best decisions we ever made in life.

"We get back to the relationships we developed, the fact that here was something that would recharge our batteries each year," he said. "It got us through all those horrible situations that life and the business world threw at us. It was something to latch onto."

And there are all those memories. Memories like the first year when Bill and his buddy overturned their canoe in a fast, rapid-filled river. Memories of who landed the biggest walleye, northern pike, brook trout and lake trout. Memories of all the evenings with fun-filled card games.

Throughout the years, there has been one important rule:

"Once we cross the Canadian border, we issue a stiff $10 fine for talking about work," he said.

Bill said his buddies drink, but not to excess. They have a few beers each night before and after dinner. He added that "apricot brandy goes great with playing cards."

The accommodations got better as the years went by. They are now staying in cabins with running, drinkable water.

The cost? Bill said it's surprisingly small. During the early years, each person paid on the average $600 to $800. It's since risen to about $1,200 to $1,400—and that includes the cost of taking the float plane out and back.

Several years ago, Bill started a custom-made fishing rod business. Everyone who makes the trip gets one of his rods.

Bill can't stress enough how this trip rejuvenated him each year and how it improved his attitude toward life in general and made him a better husband and father.

His advice for the guy who just can't see himself doing something like this?

"Don't wait. Just do it."

The Kayak Club

Three men in their early to mid-50s—Matt, Stu and Steve—met me for drinks one evening at a local restaurant to talk about their annual kayak/camping trips each fall in the Adirondack Mountains.

They hold different jobs: sales, general manager for a design firm, a banker.

The trips, they said, always take place during the second weekend after Labor Day. They leave Thursday morning and return Sunday afternoon.

They had been doing it for 18 years. They go to various primitive camping sites (no reservations needed, outhouses are the norm) and predominately use kayaks, with an occasional canoe to get there.

The group that goes each year, numbers as many as a dozen—with a constant influx or departure of guys, depending on their situations.

Stu discussed the group's beginning.

"I was 32 when I first came to the community. I started playing basketball with a few guys and we got to know each other. We were kicking around some things. I don't remember the actual moment when we came up with the idea for the trip."

He noted that Matt had his office and his kayak downtown on the lake and that probably served as an inspiration. They were two of the three original core members (one has since moved out of town). Steve joined the group a couple of years later.

Matt said he had a personal longing, a need for something like the trip. "I'm 53 now and was 35 then," he said. "I hadn't been doing anything with the guys, other than playing basketball. I love the outdoors and always wanted to do something like this.

"Truth be told, I bought a kayak and had started going up to the Adirondacks myself to use it."

Stu said the first year they went island camping on Lower Saranac Lake. It was a "whacked out group" of 12, he said, ranging from those who were "very experienced campers down to no experience."

They had fun and decided to go the next year, and the next.

Stu remembers during one of the early years, they were camped on Middle Saranac Lake, using a lean-to. Unexpectedly, four guys "in their 60s and 70s"—guys from Skaneateles, N.Y. that they did not know—appeared and wanted to share the site for the night.

No problem, he said, noting how together, how "automated" they seemed, with each knowing what to do in setting up camp and making their food.

What amazed him, he said, is these guys said they had been doing their trip for 25 straight years. "I remember thinking, *Wouldn't it be cool if we could do 25 years?*"

Over the years, Stu, the trip's main organizer, said the trip has become "formulaic." They bring in "all the essentials, including beer, coolers, box wine.

"And we eat phenomenally well. We're not limited and every year we want to do it differently. No freeze-dried food," he said.

All three men agreed the trip is food for their souls, and therapeutic in many ways. It is a well-deserved break from their work and family lives—a time of sharing, of catching up with each other, of creating memories.

Apart from the core members, there always seem to be guys coming in, or bowing out, each year. That's fine, Stu said. Occasionally, a new guy will come in with a pitch from one of the regulars. "It's often something like, 'He's been going through a hard time and he really needs something like this,'" he said

Moments of sharing occur at various, often unexpected times, Steve said, "Like when you're riding up or coming back in your cars, paddling side by side with each other in the kayaks or around the camp fire. It's funny how you often don't know what's going on (in someone's life) until those moments."

Steve said the first couple of years his wife asked, "Are you going on this trip again?"

"I was like, *Yeah!* It finally got to the point where I told her, *I'm going to be making this trip on the second weekend of September for the rest of my life, so you might as well put it on the calendar*," he said.

The Sunday Morning "Junk Run"

Rick, 61, said staying fit has been and continues to be a big part of his life.

"My job in sales often takes me out of town. Without physical fitness, my mental half doesn't work. It helps to keep the connections going."

Back in 1987 when he first moved into town, Rick and a friend began running Sunday mornings, a routine Rick had enjoyed where he lived previously. In time, they picked up another male runner. Others followed.

Today, regardless of the weather, a loose-knit group of guys gets up every Sunday and meet in front of a local restaurant. They then jog a leisurely 10K (6.2 miles) or so, depending on how they feel. Afterward, they have coffee and talk.

"We toyed with the start time. It was 7:00, then 7:30, then 6:30," he said. "Somewhere along the line we just settled on 6:41 a.m."

Rick said the guys in the group, which number more than a half dozen at times, are now all in their 50s and 60s. The pace is intentionally slow. It used to be about eight minutes a mile. Now, it has slowed to about nine minutes a mile.

"We call it a junk run," Rick said. "If anyone wants to go faster or get a workout, they do it some other time during the week. That's not what this run is about."

Rick said the early Sunday morning runs have worked out well over the years with his family life.

"You hear about these guys who get up and go play golf for 8 hours Sundays and then have drinks afterward," he said. "By doing this (the early runs), I never felt I was stealing time away from my children. Often, when I would come home, they would still be in bed. As a result, I got to spend time with them. I wanted to spend time with them."

He prefers the group thing, noting that "running alone is just boring."

At times a wife, a daughter or another local female runner has joined in the Sunday morning runs, or for the coffee time afterward. It is just not the same, though, as with the all-guy group. The chemistry, the conversation "is just different when women are there," he said.

The topics the guys talk about vary. They can be amusing, informative, even validating.

"We all have different jobs, so we don't talk work," he said. "Actually, it's like a box of chocolates each week. You never know what you're going to get. When I miss a run because of work, I'm always asking the following week, 'What did I miss?'"

In recent years, the group has come up with two traditions. During daylight saving time in the fall, the guys go that Sunday morning to a nearby state reforestation area and run an 8-mile loop through the woods.

"In addition to the coffee, we bring things like muffins, or apple crisp. When we finish running, we just circle up near our cars, eat and talk. Sometimes we're standing there shivering to death," Rick said, smiling.

The spring brings a different activity.

"When one of the guys taps his maple trees, we all go over to his house and have breakfast after our run—pancakes covered with pure maple syrup."

Horseshoes, Beer and 51 Years of Friendship

I met William and a couple of his buddies at the local bowling alley one evening for a couple of drinks, and to talk about their summer horseshoe-throwing group. He was 80, the other guys sitting around him were in their late seventies.

They said they sit at the same table every Monday evening throughout the year, drinking beer or soda, eating popcorn and talking about their families, their lives, about local happenings. It is a get-together that has its roots in a summer horseshoes group, which started 51 years ago.

William, a retired teacher with a wife and three grown daughters, said he moved to Skaneateles when he was 28. He immediately joined a men's bowling league, but was looking for more.

"I've thrown horseshoes through much of my life," he said. "I learned how to throw from my uncle. We had a camp up at the lake and that's where he taught me. There are pictures of him throwing on a beach at Guadalcanal during World War II."

William and a couple of guys from the bowling league started throwing at a neighbor's pit, and eventually at a pit William built in his backyard. When the town put a few pits plus some lights at nearby Austin Park, the group moved up there. They quickly settled into a routine that they have kept all these years.

"We start the first good Monday evening in May and throw every Monday evening through the first weekend in September," William said, adding that each time afterward they go out for a beer or two.

The guys also get together during the summer for a barbecue at least twice at one of the guy's summer camp, a short distance away. He has two horseshoe pits and the guys eat, drink and throw horseshoes there.

"At one, we eat hamburgers and hot dogs," William said. "The second one at the end of the season is a steak roast."

Are the wives and girlfriends invited?

"No, women are not allowed," he said. The same goes for the horseshoes on Monday evenings and the time afterward for beers.

"This is our time. The wives have their things, their get-togethers. We do our things. My wife is president of the local historical society. Believe me, she keeps busy."

William said at its peak, the horseshoe throwing group had as many as 16 throwers. Over the years, the numbers dwindled to about a half dozen. Guys moved, just lost interest or in some cases died.

I asked William about the tendency of men to get competitive. He said the group has not had any serious problems with that, stressing that horseshoes has just been an excuse to get together all these years.

"This is about socializing. Men need to socialize and it helps to have a group like this. It's good for your mental health," he said. "Those who don't have anything, any outside groups they belong to, are missing out on a lot."

To make everyone comfortable and keep things on a level playing field at the horseshoe pits, William said, he and the others came up with a handicap system in which they spotted the weaker players a certain amount of points each game.

William stressed the group always meets afterward for beer, even if the horseshoes get canceled due to bad weather. That is part of their 51-year tradition.

What's ahead for the horseshoe group?

"It's gotten to the point that with sore shoulders and sore arms, we all now take a big step forward (about three feet closer to the opposite pit) before we throw," he said. "We joke about when it's going to come to the point when we're just throwing bean bags."

It's In The Cards

Jim, 78, a retired banker, said he has been playing poker with his buddies a long time.

"Let's see, I was invited to play in the group back in 1973. I was 38 at the time. Been playing ever since. That would make it more than 40 years."

Jim said the group tries to play every Friday night, though sickness, vacations and other personal obligations over the years has cut into their playing time. "And we don't play on Good Friday, or over the Christmas holidays."

Early on it was just nickel-and-dime action. Then, the stakes rose to a quarter, a half dollar.

"We got into some wild games with lots of wild cards," he said. "Over time, we got to playing just straight poker games."

The stakes gradually climbed, but were then reduced to make sure everyone could afford it. Currently, the buy-in for a night of playing is $50.

Jim pointed out the group has a long-standing tradition of taking quarters or half dollars out of the pot and putting it aside in *a kitty*. At year's end, the kitty money is donated to a local charity. Past amounts have been in the $300 to $500 range, he said.

The poker group currently includes another banker, a fireman, an optician, a hospital administrator, a pharmacist and a businessman—all retirees.

"It's my night out with the guys. You let your hair down. It's very relaxing," Jim said. "The wives support it. They know where you are. You're not out in bars, not out chasing women."

I asked him if the money ever got in the way of a good time.

"The most I ever won in a single night was $1,200, and that was with two guys who I'd never met before," he said. "They never came back."

There was a lesson learned. "Generally, we pick people with similar interests, who we can get along with," he said. "We're not in it for the money. If we find someone's playing is questionable or getting too intense, they're never invited again."

Jim said the group's players over the years have all been working guys, with salaries coming in. The money to play "never came out of their family budgets."

"Most players had their own poker fund that they tapped into," he said.

The group's players have grown close as friends. They have done business with each other, participated in community service and fund-raising events together.

Jim remembers the wedding of one of the player's daughters.

"The whole club got invited and we were seated at the reception at our own table," he said. "In the middle of the table was a deck of cards. We played for about an hour. It certainly attracted a lot of attention. All the money on the table ended up going to the bride."

It Helps When Someone Takes the Lead

There is a lot of inertia out there among men "to remain in whatever state they're in and not move out of it," said Nick as he sipped a cup of coffee during breakfast at a local diner.

"There are not a lot of good models in our culture for men taking care of themselves," he added. "So it does take a mover usually to get something going, and keep it going."

Nick, 58, a journalist, was talking about his annual getaway with three other guys during the past 13 years. The men have traveled to a number of different locations and enjoyed an impressive array of exciting and interesting activities together.

They have cycled through the Finger Lakes, cross county skied in Vermont, ocean kayaked in Maine, hiked and camped at such locations as Grand Canyon in Nevada, Arches National Park in Wyoming and Moab National Park in Utah, snorkeled in St. John in the Caribbean—even gone to Las Vegas, which included time on a house boat on nearby Lake Mead.

The key organizer? It is the wife of one of the men. She picks the spot each year, makes all the arrangements and reservations and pays for the group's lodgings. It is all part of a unique Christmas gift that she gives annually to her husband.

It is up to the guys to get there, pay for their food and whatever else they choose to do—which often are activities the wife has selected for them.

"She's a beautiful spirit. A beautiful woman," Nick said. "She asked for nothing from us. She's continually praised and adored—and thanked."

Nick said the group's three core members, who are all within a few years age-wise of each other, are childhood buddies. All three lost their fathers at an early age and all worked as counselors for a camping/hiking program for troubled youth in Massachusetts. All have children.

The three all grew up in Central New York. Time and careers, though, spread them around. One, a surgeon, lives in Chicago. Nick lives in Syracuse, N.Y. The other, a chief executive officer for a non-profit agency, lives in Michigan.

The three touched bases with each over the years—at weddings, parties or when visiting relatives. It was the surgeon's idea to take things to another level. He suggested the three take a bike trip.

Nick said he took the lead and organized a four-day bike trip throughout the Finger Lakes, arranging the lodgings and other particulars. A fourth friend joined them for the final dinner at the Aurora Inn on the shore of Cayuga Lake.

"It was a powerful trip. We took some risks—some emotional risks," Nick said. "Somebody shared a poem that meant a lot to them. It was about raising a daughter."

The momentum continued. The second year was an Adirondack hike. The third, a cross country ski trip in Vermont. But work, family and things such as kids graduating from high school got in the way and the annual getaway trip stopped.

More than a year passed. To everyone's surprise, Nick said, the wife of the surgeon stepped in. She is a physician as well.

"She realized the connections made on the previous trips for her husband were so important. She understood what it meant to him, their marriage and that he really needed something like this," he said.

She arranged a hiking trip in Maine, which included time for ocean kayaking "She found accommodations, paid for them and gifted us with that," he said.

Was there any hesitation on the part of the other guys to go?

"No, it seemed like a no-brainer," Nick said. "The offer was there to stay at a lodge on the ocean. There was the ocean kayaking. All we had to do was get there. The rooms were reserved, paid for. So, in a sense, she became a partner in it."

What she recognized, he said, was that the excursion had to include a sense of "boyishness. It had to be more than just meeting for a weekend and sitting around in a lodge. It had to involve activity, something physically demanding in a certain way. That helped."

During the past several years, the annual trip continues to grow in importance and take on new dimensions to those who go. A fourth guy has joined. Several other friends have been invited. Themes have been developed beforehand, readings get shared. Yoga has been weaved into the trip's daily routine. (Nick is also a yoga instructor)

One thing that never ceases to amaze him, Nick said, is how there always seems to be other guys they run into while on these trips—guys who, when they find out what is going on, readily engage in conversation and share intimate thoughts and observations about themselves. Often, something that is said by those individuals continues to be discussed by the four for the rest of the trip.

Moments like that, Nick said, reveals a real need among these men—and others as well.

"They want to drink from the cup, too."

Afterthoughts

The guys mentioned above got me thinking about my life back in my late 20s and early 30s, when Laura and I lived for more than seven years in Southeast Los Angeles. This was before our daughter and son came into our lives.

I am often asked by friends and acquaintances what I miss most about those days. Was it the warm, sunny weather? The beaches? The diversity, the culture and entertainment—the food?

None of the above. I miss my friends, particularly my buddies from Cerritos United, a recreational soccer team.

I was working then as a reporter at a newspaper. My wife was an employment consultant. Initially, we were hurting for friends. I had a cousin and her husband living north of us in Bakersfield (a three-hour drive away), and there was a good childhood friend of Laura's who lived in nearby Santa Monica.

Both our families were back in Upstate New York, and we used up much of our vacation time jetting back home each holiday season. We missed a lot being so far away from home—weddings, funerals, babies, graduations, and family get-togethers.

In time, we connected with people in our apartment complex and with folks at our jobs. Then Laura joined a women's soccer team. I ended up joining Cerritos United, which included several of the husbands/boyfriends of the women on Laura's team.

Our relationships and our closeness to the people on those two teams took off. With the good weather out in Los Angeles, soccer is played year-round, and we both played nearly every week.

It was not long before we were both going out separately with our respective teammates after practices. Following the games each Sunday, members of both teams would also rendezvous for pizza and beer, or meet at someone's house for a late afternoon party.

That evolved into team Halloween parties, New Year's parties and birthday parties for teammates' children. In addition, there were weddings, baptisms, helping each other with home or car repairs, being there for each other during happy and sad moments—all the closeness, favors and experiences that good friends share.

My team had practice Tuesday and Thursday evenings, with time always set aside afterward for beer, pizza and conversation at the local Shakey's Pizza restaurant. I laugh when I think about all the free beer we finagled out of waitresses and new managers, claiming it was one of our birthdays that night, or that we were entitled to a free pitcher after every four we polished off.

"We've been coming here for years. The old manager always did that," was our line. It usually worked.

Those were fun and memorable times. The crazy thing about it all was that I had to be at the newspaper the following morning at 6:30 a.m., typing up obituaries.

One Tuesday evening I decided to skip practice following a heavy rainstorm. One of the senior team members, Pio, who was Peruvian, later set me straight. He noted the other guys had gone to Shakey's that Tuesday evening and I had missed it.

"If you're going to be a part of this team, you have to remember one thing: No matter what, you tell Laura there's always soccer practice on Tuesday and Thursday nights—and you come," he said.

I understood and rarely missed *practice* from that point on.

Things changed after we left Los Angeles to come back to the East Coast. There were three job changes and moves, along with two children to raise. For years, I yearned for that closeness with the guys that I had out in Los Angeles. Nothing came close to the feelings I had for those soccer buddies—until recently.

Granted, there will never be another Cerritos United for me. My knees are shot and I am terribly out of shape. Two nights of practice each week is definitely out of the question.

Pio's words, though, continue to resonate. It was not about the soccer. It was about committing to time with good friends.

CHAPTER 15

ADVICE TO WOMEN ABOUT MAKING US HAPPY

Love is that condition in which the happiness of another person is essential to your own.
~ Robert A. Heinlein, science fiction writer

Happiness is not something ready-made. It comes from your own actions.
~ Dalai Lama, spiritual leader of the Tibetan people

What makes me happy? It's a number of things.

It is being spoken to, and listened to with respect (not being talked at). It is all about being included, and having an equal say in financial and social decisions in our marriage. It is acting as a team with my wife when dealing with our kids.

It is also recognition that sex is, and continues to be, a very important part of my life. A hot meal at dinner every once in a while doesn't hurt, either. It is having, and being encouraged to have, my own space with male friends.

Finally, I like someone who laughs (and makes me laugh), is spontaneous and is not afraid to try something new.

I asked the following guys what advice they would they give to women on the topic of making middle-aged men happy. Their comments follow:

> We need our ego stroked before any other part of our anatomy. Also, avoid headaches.
> ~ Neal, 53, lawyer, married

To keep your man happy and at home, talk less and listen more. You hear men don't want to talk about their feelings. That's not true. They have a hard time, but they often get debated rather than listened to.
~ Mike, 55, counselor, married

Whether you like it or not, be up for sex—a lot. Be cheerful for the most part. Not be threatened by the fact I have a lot of attractive women who are friends. Don't hold grudges. Allow us (men) to apologize and accept it.
~ Steve, 55, entertainment manager, married

Don't forget to treat him like he's important. And you can turn this either way. Don't make him feel stupid for still feeling like a kid. Don't tell him you're too old for that. Surprise him. Be imaginative. One day I came home, it was around my birthday. I went to bed, and then went to the bathroom and came back. Candles were lit and this and that. Out comes this massage oil and this plastic thing, this massage tool. Doing that, it was just like … wow! You know, something simple like that. It doesn't have to evolve into a sexual encounter, but it piqued my interest.
~ Fritz, 51, truck driver, divorced

I would say be open to new friends and new experiences. Avoid using the bedroom as an emotional tool. If you're angry at 4 p.m. and still angry later than night, it'll carry over into the bedroom and into other parts of your relationship.
~ Al, 55, painting contractor, married

Have a good sense of humor. Be happy. Avoid lying, hurting people and not working together on

problems. Work together if you have problems. That's what I ask for in a person. Be truthful to me. Don't bullshit me.
~ Hugh, 50, insurance man, divorced

Give us space when we need it. Butter us up when we need it. Give us a hug when we need it, too.
~ Ivan, 54, college professor, married

If a guy is going to stray, he is going to stray. The woman can't really stop it, even if she had a 20-inch waist line. What can she do? Start with the correct man.
~ Henry, 58, financial consultant, married

It works both ways. She has to keep telling him that she loves him, and vice versa. I think it's more doing as much as saying. It's stroking your ego. Like, I'm proud of what you said today. And when she's stroking your ego (it works both ways), you spend more time together, the intimacy and all that grows. But you still have to have your own space. You can't be smothering each other.
~ Cliff, 53, architect, married

Avoid being a nag. Give us room to be ourselves, to do what we want, to make a card club or a horseshoe club or to go golfing on weekends. Refrain from gaining too much weight. Don't become sloppy. (Women) should feel proud of themselves and act accordingly. (They should) maintain a high self-esteem for men to continue to feel they're attractive. Avoid becoming complacent about their husband, about their life, about their family. Avoid becoming complacent about life. Avoid that at all costs.
~ Vic, 55, middle school teacher, married

I think there's non-sexual things that keep men happy, and there's sexual things that keep them happy. I think guys expect women to do their part. Take on the housewife role—the basic stuff, the cooking, the cleaning, the laundry, taking care of the stuff the guy doesn't necessarily want to do—the typical division of labor… not that there's a strict brick wall between who does what, but generally speaking, take care of the kids, keep them safe, educated and supervised.
~ Sid, 52, businessman, married

They should show interest in what the man in their life is doing. Please have some interest, concern—genuine concern. You don't have to have sex. I know it would be nice, but it shouldn't be the main thing in a relationship. It should come as a reward for having a nice relationship. To keep him home, show him some love, have some interest. That's all.
~ Tracy, 52, office manager, married

I have no complaints with my wife. I like to run. If I want to do a race, she tells me to just go. My advice is don't keep your husband prisoner. Know what he needs to do to keep happy and encourage him to do it. Usually with me it's something outdoors.
~ Rick, 61, sales, married

Satisfy him sexually and if you take care of his cooking and cleaning and maintain his house environment for him, those are two great things. And that third, that you do the same things he does, or (at least) take an interest. If I'm playing video games, and you play video games, that's great. Or if I like riding motorcycles, and you like riding motorcycles, that's great. To not be interested in anything I do is a total drag.

Finally, don't nag him. It's so annoying when my wife nags me about not picking up my clothes, or spending too much time doing something I enjoy. It's just like, you want something and I only have a limited amount of time, and you're nagging me because I haven't done something. That's the biggest thing.

~ Sam, 49, accountant, married

Avoid trying to manipulate everything (we) do. When you get married, you like your wife; she likes you. If she changes you, you're not the same person who she fell in love with in the beginning. Why would she want to change that?

~ Bob, 47, mechanic, married

I think they have to treat us with the same respect that they're expecting us to show them. And I don't think that happens. I think a lot of women's attitudes are based on what I call the sitcom male. We're not all morons, like the guys on Seinfeld and the rest of them.

~ Clyde, 50, small business owner, divorced

You can't put demands on a guy. I don't do well with lots of demands. Don't tell me we're going shopping, we're going to the mall Saturday… don't ever tell me what to do. You can ask me, you can coax me. If I don't even know I'm being coaxed, I'm okay. My time is valuable to me.

Also, with me (don't limit) my social life. I have lots of friends and I have female friends. Women can be very insecure about that. I've been around 50 years. For a long time, you know. I know people. I need

people. When somebody tells me there's people who I can and can't talk to, you can go bye-bye.
~ Ian, 50, web page designer, divorced

Do things together. Interesting things. Things you both like. And good sex. It isn't always about quantity, but quality. To avoid him, to ignore him. To not have sex with him—that's trouble.
~ Jeremy, 52, retail manager, widowed

Well, I can't speak for the general public, but I know what works in our marriage, which would be trust, love… that's all part of it… friendship, caring; those are probably the big hitters.
~ Jack, 50, businessman, married

Don't waste your time trying to get people who are middle-aged to be something they're not. It's almost like that show, "I Love You, You're Perfect—Now Change." Sometimes, you just get that feeling when you're out with other people… some women are still trying to make their spouses into something they're not. My advice would just be: Let em be. Don't try to change them. All you're going to create is a lot of antagonism.
~ Scott, 60, retired teacher, married

Don't avoid your relationship, or not make it a priority. Make it a priority. Yes, I know we men are sometimes stupid, shallow. But you have women who spend 190 percent of their free time with the kids and don't even notice their husband is there. Yes, the kids are your focus, but it's very important to continue nurturing your relationship (with your man).
It's like that old saying about being on an airplane (that's about to crash). Put your oxygen mask on first

(for your relationship) before you tend to your children. Because if you don't, you're not going to be able to help your children. You're going to end up not having a full family unit that takes care of the children.

Finally, it's about communicating, really understanding your guy. Understanding where he is. Not where you think he is, but where he really is. Is it athletics? Is it sex? Everybody, every guy is a little different in his top priorities. Is it going away for a weekend and getting a bottle of champagne, watching movies? Get close enough to the guy to understand what his kicks are. Find out what gives him a kick. Go find out. Go investigate. Go spend the time because a lot of couples have gotten to the point where it's not even possible to have that kind of discussion.

~ Frank, 55, carpenter, divorced

Afterthoughts

That last comment by Frank, "a lot of couples have gotten to the point where it's not even possible to have that kind of discussion," describes how I was starting to feel before writing this book.

That was before the marriage counseling, before I regained some balance in my life with friends and outside activities and before I took a risk and accepted the outdoors writing job for the newspaper.

I asked the question to give guys a chance to speak directly to women without being interrupted or judged. It reminded me of moments during our marriage counseling where one of us was given space to start and finish a point, while the other was reminded to be quiet and listen.

Many of the guys hedged in their answers, saying things like, "Of course, this has to go both ways," or

"Marriage and any relationship are all about compromises."

Other common refrains were: "Yeah, but you know how it really is in a marriage: *If momma isn't happy, nobody's happy*. Or, *If everyone around me is happy, I'm happy*."

Steve, the married banker whom I quoted in the last chapter about his annual kayak/camping trips with his buddies, put things in perspective.

"They say, *Happy wife, happy life*. That's right. But nobody wants a disgruntled husband bumming around the house."

Frankly, there is no one, perfect answer to my question, no handy checklist I can provide. Middle-aged men, depending on their personalities, their situations, and their philosophies of life, have a wide variety of needs.

There is one thing, though, that I do feel confident in saying to middle-aged women and men alike: Have that conversation that Frank, the carpenter, talked about.

When you do, be open, honest and respectful to each other. Listen closely to what the other person says about their needs and desires. Paraphrase (reflect) what they say back to them so that they know you understand.

Finally, and most importantly, cover all the bases (that includes sex) and resolve to take action.

The other option is to seek marriage counseling. Pursuing outside help is not an admission of failure or weakness. It reflects a sincere and positive desire to make things better.

Relationships, like your car or truck, occasionally need to be fine-tuned, or even overhauled from time to time. Things change. You move to a new location as a result of a job change. Kids grow up and leave. Your love life loses its spark.

It helps to have an experienced counselor steer the conversation and act as a sounding board. Think of him or her as an emotional mechanic.

Mike, a licensed marriage counselor, told me it is often harder for guys to admit they need counseling and to seek it. Men, by their nature, like to fix things, he said. They feel guilty about a troubled relationship and often as a defense mechanism, resort to a *blame game* mentality.

"But deep down most guys feel it's their role to make their wife happy and it hurts to think about failing to do that," he said.

Women, he said, frequently have a more positive approach to marriage counseling, seeing it as an opportunity. He said they can help their male partner going into it by emphasizing that counseling is not about guilt or assigning blame, but about embarking on *collaboration* to make the relationship better.

Mike said it often helps to revisit certain things with couples such as: "Why did we get together in the first place? What was our vision back then for our relationship? What is it now? How did we play with each other back then? How do we play together now?"

For us, marriage counseling was a godsend. We heard each other out, voiced a renewed enthusiasm for our relationship and made some much-needed changes. I can honestly say my love and appreciation for Laura is stronger than ever.

There are no guarantees, though. You might not like what you hear. Some relationships just are not meant to be. It is better to find that out now as opposed to continuing to suffer in silence, or to keep fooling yourself that somehow, some way, things will just work themselves out.

Whether it is between yourselves or with the help of a counselor, do yourself a favor and have that conversation.

Life is a gift. It is within your power to begin the second half of yours with happiness, passion and optimism—or not.

EPILOGUE

The man who views the world at fifty the same as he did at twenty has wasted thirty years of his life.
~ Muhammad Ali, former world heavyweight boxing champion

For the past 33 years, I have looked in the mirror every morning and asked myself, "If today were the last day of my life, would I do what I am about to do today?" And whenever the answer has been "No" for too many days in a row, I know I need to change something.
~ Steve Jobs, entrepreneur, inventor, co-founder of Apple Inc.

I sat in my theater seat at Syracuse Stage surrounded by women on all sides. It was the production, *Menopause, the Musical.* My wife had bought tickets a couple of months prior.

Before the show began, a woman took center stage and began welcoming groups of women that had come together. The women cheered, clapped—shrieked. They were there on a *girls' night out.*

I was one of three men in the audience that weekday night. I found the show hilarious. There were lots of songs from the 1960s and 1970s with the words rewritten to focus on hot flashes, loss of memory, the thickening of thighs.

"Cha—cha—change. Change of life," the four women on stage sang to the popular Motown classic, *Chain of Fools.*

The theme was simple. Menopause happens. You simply learn to live with the hot flashes, laugh about it, accept it—and as the grand finale song demands, women have to adopt *A New Attitude*.

So what about the guys?

There is no menopausal or universal wakeup. At times the mid-life years feel like a gradual decay, a grinding slog with no end in sight. You hear things like the 60s are the new 40s. You shake your head at all the *Viagra* and *Cialis* commercials, and wonder why you are always feeling the need to take a pee.

You just put your head down and keep going.

The reality is that for most of us, our lives are half over—actually more than half over. The average life span of a male in this country is 76.3 years, according to the U.S. Department of Health and Human Services. For a woman, it's 81.1 years. [17]

Throughout my 40s and entering my 50s, I was questioning my life. Is this as good as it gets? Can't I do better?

Talking to other men helped. Often their words sparked a new attitude in me, a willingness to embrace change in positive ways as opposed to seeking a quick, ill-advised fix. Sometimes it took a hard, unexpected turn of events, a crisis, to put things in perspective.

One came the day I was in a hospital bed at Community General Hospital in Syracuse holding my wife's hand, quietly praying and awaiting the results of several tests.

They were tests to determine why I had collapsed in a sudden moment of dizziness in our bedroom that morning… why my face immediately turned beat red… why I started sweating bullets and began puking in the toilet. It was dry heave after dry heave.

I could not stand up. I was scared. Scared it was heart or stroke related. I was petrified that my life was about to take a horrible, twisted turn.

Laura drove me to the hospital emergency room. The morning was a blur as I was pricked, probed, X-Rayed and closely monitored. A nurse told me later in the day that a CAT scan had found "a suspicious spot" on the right, front side of my brain. That test was followed by an MRI, along with an ultrasound of my carotid arteries.

Suddenly all of life's problems and worries seemed miniscule, with the exception of one—my health. After nearly seven hours in the hospital, a doctor came back with news.

"All clear," she said. "The spot on your brain was nothing. Your carotids are clear. Your heart is okay. You had an episode of what we believe was viral vertigo," she continued, adding it would clear up by itself. She prescribed a drug to help with the nausea and dizziness—and I was sent home, tired and ravaged by hours of puking and worry.

It was a wake-up call. A grim reminder that I could not take my health—or anything else in my life—for granted.

Highlights during the past several years include:

Leveling With My Wife about the Status of Our Marriage

It was a situation prompted by several things: social loneliness, my perception that she did not respect me or my wishes enough, screwed up communication patterns between us, troubles in the bedroom—and a deep-seated feeling that she was taking me for granted.

We went through marriage counseling and ironed out a lot of wrinkles. Today I feel I get a lot more love, appreciation and respect from my wife. I try my best to give it back to her. Our sex life remains vibrant and mutually satisfying. I arrange at least two overnight getaways a year, which is a change from when Laura would always schedule everything.

We made a vow to each other on our wedding day: "I want you to grow old with me, for the best is yet to be." I still feel that is true.

Life is full of distractions, especially during the child-rearing years and with all the stress of work and careers. Still, your relationship with your partner needs to be constantly tended to and given the attention it truly deserves.

I was reminded of the importance of that during a funeral service for the wife of one of my cousins.

Standing up near the end of the Mass, one of my cousin's daughters recalled how supportive and loving her parents had been to her and her sisters during their childhood. She added that the idea of her parents being "a couple"—of being lovers, of having passion for each other—was off her radar screen. She said they were "always just Mom and Dad."

She began to see things differently as she grew older and got into a relationship herself. Watching her father at her mom's bedside every day for the final two weeks of her life, "holding her hand, caressing her hair and face and repeatedly telling her that he loved her" opened her eyes even more. Apart from the kids, there was also "something separate, something special" between her parents.

She told those in the church that she will always try to remember that, and will work hard to maintain that in her relationship.

I could not have said it better.

Making New Friends

This was huge, as big as the changes I made involving my marriage.

Despite having a ton of acquaintances after more than two decades in journalism, I felt depressed and lonely. I had no best friend who I regularly talked to, went fishing with—or anything. I was not taking care of myself.

Almost nine years later, my decision to follow the advice on my note card—*It won't happen unless I do it*—has paid off—not only for me, but for the other guys involved.

The Co-ed Volleyball Team

The Skantown Strikers has been going strong for eight years, though the personnel has changed considerably due to injuries and other reasons. In fairness to Fred, whom I mentioned in the opening chapter of this book, we did start going out occasionally as a team, and we have had several post-season, potluck dinners.

After getting injured in indoor soccer, Laura joined the volleyball team. She has been on it now for four years. Laura and I go out for a beer and wings afterward. It has become our little date each week, and we look forward to it. Occasionally our teammates join us.

Laura will often drive me home afterward and catch up with her indoor soccer buddies at another bar in town for an hour or so, and that's fine by me. We're both getting what we need.

The Poker Group

We are celebrating our eighth year together. We rotate the games around each other's houses and meet the second Saturday evening of each month.

Positive spin-offs have included:

A three-day, fall camping/fishing trip in the Adirondacks.

One of the group's members has opened his cottage on Lake George for a weekend getaway for the couples each fall that includes a Saturday night game of poker for the guys, while the ladies go out on the town. It's become a tradition.

We also get together as couples around Valentine's Day with the guys orchestrating things. Outings have included dinner dances, dinners prepared by the men and a musical concert.

Helping each other out. We helped one member tear down his back porch and participated in a "painting party" at another's residence. Add to that, advice, time and help on various home projects and car repairs.

Finally, two couples, who were not friends before the group was formed, vacationed together on a memorable trip to the Grand Canyon and Las Vegas.

The Skaneateles Horseshoe International Team

This group is on its seventh year.

It reminds me at times of my old Cerritos United soccer team, with its fun and constant kidding around. We refer to each other as *The Brethren.*

The group purchased a plaque with the names of winners from the past summer seasons that hangs on the wall at a local bar. There is also a funny-looking trophy that each season's champ is obliged to display "in a prominent place in his home" throughout the year that he reigns.

Add to that hilarious email newsletters, all the funny nicknames and off-the-wall conversations that more than once have had me in tears from laughing so hard.

We have a team doctor (he's actually a chiropractor), a team chaplain (he's a Quaker, who only believes in silent prayer), a team humorist/grammarian (he's entertained and educated us by reading racy definitions from the Urban Dictionary)—and of course, the all-knowing Commissioner, who initially set the whole thing up. And yes, there are written bylaws.

What started as a summertime activity, has been gradually evolving into a year-round scene, including all-guys dinner/movie outings, attendance at Syracuse

University basketball games, a New Year's party and wine-tasting outings with the wives. The activities and the connections between the guys continue to grow. Several of the guys in the group joined a local service club together.

One guy's wife set up a celebration for her man's 50th birthday. She arranged, and paid for, an all-guys outing at an indoor, high speed go-cart outing at the local shopping mall—and then afterward footed the bill for The Brethren's first round of beer at a nearby pub afterward.

Since getting involved in the above activities with guys, I have heard from several friends and family members that I may have gone a little overboard with things. I disagree, noting these relationships and the time I've spent with friends has considerably enriched my life.

My initial emphasis was a bit selfish. I simply wanted to achieve parity with my wife when it came to spending time with friends. Ed, the husband of one of my cousins, who does marriage counseling, voiced caution.

"It seems to me you two are in a nuclear arms race to see who can spend the most time away from each other," he said, raising the possibility that divorce could be in our future.

That struck a chord. After that conversation I had a new focus. It became more than just making myself happy. It was about achieving balance—balancing my marriage with my personal and social needs. I stopped resenting, and began encouraging Laura to be with her friends. I received the same support from her.

Today we both have our regular outside activities with friends, but have scaled back a little. Our relationship remains our top priority.

Taking a Risk in My Job, Embracing the Outdoors

For more than 23 years I was a reporter and editor on the city desk, responsible for covering hard news, politics, crime, and investigative reporting. Then along came the outdoors job on the newspaper. Taking it was a risk, a risk in the prime of my journalism career. I could have crashed and burned. I made it work.

Looking back, it was a great fit with my experience, and with my personality. It played to all my strengths.

I remember my son, Alex, coming home a couple of years afterward from dinner at a friend's house and being told by the girl's father that he religiously read my column in the newspaper.

"His dad thinks you're some kind of hunting god or something," he said, laughing. "If they only knew."

It is true. I've only been hunting for a few years. I have two deer to my credit. When you are covering everything from birding to bear hunting, there are a lot of subject areas to learn about and to experience for the first time.

I have come to realize the outdoors can be a salve, an antidote for life's worries. Much of it for me is brand new. I tell people often that when I am fishing, hunting, hiking, camping—whatever—I feel like a little kid in a middle-aged man's body.

About a year before I took the outdoors job, when I was really feeling down about things, my friend Chris took me up on a spur-of-the-moment offer to do a late spring fishing/camping trip in the Adirondacks. He did not question my reason for wanting to do it. I just told him that work was driving me nuts and I had to get away.

We drove up to Lake Lila on a cold, drizzly Saturday morning. After packing our canoe to the point where it was almost sinking, we paddled about a mile on the lake against wind and 2-3-foot waves to an idyllic little island and set up camp. The rain stopped.

We built a roaring campfire (we had brought our own wood) and prepared a delicious meal of steak, with potatoes wrapped in aluminum foil and cooked in the fire's coals and some canned green beans—washing it all down with plenty of beer.

That night, for the first time with anyone, I talked about what I was going through in my marriage, my career, my life in general. I was miserable, in need of change, of some sort of fix, I said. Chris patiently listened, occasionally offering good advice. On the way home, Chris noted the outing was good for him as well, and that we should make it a yearly thing.

For seven years after, our annual fall fishing/camping trips took us to several different locations throughout the Adirondacks. We had all sorts of experiences, caught lots of fish and hunted and started some crazy traditions. We unwound. We bolstered each other.

I felt those trips would go on forever. God had other plans. Chris died in late 2012, the victim of cancer. I miss him a ton. I often think back to that cold evening around the roaring camp fire on Lake Lila. I can still hear Chris's words as we sipped our beers.

"You know, it just doesn't get any better than this."

A Meaningful Birthday

I wrote early on in this book about the stark differences between my 40th and 50th birthdays. I am ending it with my 60th birthday, and the events around that day. There was no party, no big celebration and no memorable gifts. The morning I turned 60, I was at the funeral of Jim Downs, my beloved father-in-law.

I delivered his eulogy. I talked about Jim's life, which spanned 88 years. I covered it all—his military experience, job, family life and his friends.

Jim had a solid core of friends, many who he had stayed close to since high school. He vacationed, bowled, played cards and golfed with many of them for years. He particularly liked to golf. My mother-in-law, June, made sure Jim was wearing his golf-themed tie in the casket.

One of the last persons at the viewing before the funeral Mass was Jim's life-long golfing buddy, Eli. He had played a round with Jim the summer before, their last time together on the links.

I watched as Eli paused before the casket and bowed his head. He then reached inside his suit coat pocket and pulled out a golf ball, placing it on Jim's chest. He said goodbye to his buddy and walked away.

That day and the next were filled with family gatherings, lots of food and numerous stories about Jim. I tried my best to be there for Laura. However, I began feeling headachy. My throat was getting sore. It was time for me to head for home.

As I was driving back with my daughter, Katie, I returned a call from Tom, one of my poker buddies who was unable to make the service. He expressed his condolences and told me that Skaneateles had received about 12 inches of snow.

"Oh great. I haven't been home for several days," I said. "I'm coming down with a goddamn cold. It'll be really fun shoveling all that snow. There's probably a three-foot-high pile from the plow at the entrance to my driveway."

I then changed the subject, offering more specifics about the funeral and how Laura and her mother were doing. A little more than an hour later at 10 p.m., I turned down our street. Our driveway came into view.

"Look Dad, angels did it," my daughter said.

The 90-foot long, 20-foot wide, sloped driveway had been completely shoveled. At the top, near the garage door, we found a small bag with a Tupperware container filled with a tasty stew and a card.

Tom and Jeff, my poker buddies, had rushed over on a moment's notice on that cold, snowy Friday night and shoveled my driveway. Tom's wife had supplied the stew.

All I could think of at that moment was, *the guys were there for me!* I vowed I would do the same for them some day. That night in bed, I could not help but dwell on the shoveled driveway, and about that golf ball on my father-in-law's chest.

The message was clear: Good friends make for a good life.

SOURCES

Chapter 3:

1. Julie Scelfo, "Men and Depression (Facing Darkness)," Newsweek, Feb. 26, 2007
2. AARP Magazine. "The Divorce Experience: A Study of Divorce at Midlife and Beyond," May 2004
3. Anne Fisher, "Boys vs. Girls: What's Behind the College Grad Gender Gap?" **management.fortune.cnn.com**, March 27, 2013
4. U.S. Bureau of Labor Statistics, "Women in the Labor Force: A Databook," February 2013
5. Catherine Rampell, "Women on the Rise as Family Breadwinner," The New York Times, May 29, 2013
6. Sabrina Taverise, The New York Times. "Married Couples are No Longer a Majority, Census Finds," May 26, 2011

Chapter 4

7. Alice G. Walton, Forbes magazine, "The Gender Inequality of Suicide: Why are Men at Such High Risk?" Sept. 24, 2012
8. Katie Drummond, AOL news, "Suicide Rate Greater Among Divorce Men, Research Finds," March 9, 2010

Chapter 5

9. Gail Sheehy, *The New Passages*, Ballantine Books, New York, 1995, page 274
10. Mayo Clinic Health Solutions bulletin, November 2007 issue. "Why Men Need Friends."

Chapter 7

11. Gail Sheehy, *Sex and the Seasoned Woman – Pursuing the Passionate Life*, Random House, New York, 2006
12. Andersen, Christopher P., *Jagger unauthorized*, Delacore Press, Bantam Doubleday Dell Publishing Group, Inc. New York 1993, page 333

Chapter 13

13. Pew Research Religion and Public Life survey, 2012, "'Nones' on the Rise," Oct. 9, 2012, www.pewforum.org.
14. David Murrow, *Why Men Hate Going to Church*, David Murrow Nelson Books, Nashville, Tenn., 2004

15. Gary Gunderson and Larry Pray, *Leading Causes of Life (Five Fundamentals to Change the Way You Live Your Life)*, Abingdon Press, Nashville, Tenn., 2004, page 54 (Used by permission)
16. Rick Warren, *The Purpose Driven Life*, Zondervan Publishers, Grand Rapids, Mich., 2002, page 139

Epilogue

17. U.S. Department of Health and Human Services, National Vital Statistics Reports, "Deaths: Preliminary Data for 2011," Oct. 10, 2012

Quotes at the beginnings of chapters were found on **brainyquote.com, quotery.com, thinkexist.com, aquotes.net, quonation.com and **goodreads.com**

READING LIST

John Gray, *Men are from Mars, Women are from Venus*, HarperCollins Publishers, New York, 1992

John Gray, *Venus on Fire, Mars on Ice (Hormonal Balance – The Key to Life, Love and Energy)*, Mind Publishing Inc., Coquitlam, British Columbia, Canada, 2010

Gail Sheehy, *The New Passages*, Ballantine Books, New York, 1995

Gail Sheehy, *Sex and the Seasoned Woman – Pursuing the Passionate Life* Random House, New York, 2006

Howell Raines, *Fly Fishing Through the Midlife Crisis*, William Morrow and Company, Inc., New York, 1993

Susan Faludi, *Stiffed, The Betrayal of the American Man*, HarperCollins Books, New York, 1999

Mike Dugan, *Men Fake Foreplay... And Other Lies That are True*, Holtzbrinck Publishers, 2004

Diamond Dallas Page, *Yoga for Regular Guys*, Quirk Books, Philadelphia, 2005

Steve Chapman, *The Good Husband's Guide to Balancing Hobbies and Marriage,* Harvest House Publishers, Eugene, Oregon, 2005

Charla Muller, with Betsy Thorpe, *365 Nights (A Memoir of Intimacy)*, Berkeley Books, New York, 2008

Michael F. Roizen, *Real Age (Are You as Young as You Can Be?)*, HarperCollins Publishers, 2000

Hanna Rosen, *The End of Men (And the Rise of Women)*, Riverhead Books, New York, New York, 2012

Eric Klinenberg, *Going Solo, (The Extraordinary Rise and Appeal of Living Alone)*, The Penguin Press, New York, 2012

Garrison Keillor, *The Book of Guys*, Penguin Books, New York, 1993

Rick Warren, *The Purpose Driven Life*, Zondervan Publishers, Grand Rapids, Mich., 2002

David Murrow, *Why Men Hate Going to Church*, Nelson Books, Nashville, Tenn., 2005

Gary Gunderson and Larry Pray, *Leading Causes of Life. Five Fundamentals to Change the Way You Live Your Life*, Abingdon Press, Nashville, 2009

Michael Korda, *Man to Man (Surviving Prostate Cancer)*, Random House, New York, 1997

Robert Bly, *Iron John, A Book About Men*, Addison-Wesley Publishing Co., Inc., New York, 1990

Sam Keen, *Fire in the Belly (On Being a Man)*, Bantam Books, New York, 1991

Final note: *Even though my daughter, Katie, thinks it's the corniest country song ever written, I highly recommend listening closely to the words of Tim McGraw's song, "Live Like You Were Dying."*

David J. Figura – *Author Biography*

David J. Figura describes himself as "your average middle age guy who loves the outdoors, sports and his beer. I'm also balding, fighting the battle of the gut, taking high blood pressure medication and getting nagged by my wife and daughter to use teeth-whitening strips," he says.

A Cornell University graduate, David is an award-winning journalist with more than 30 years of experience as a reporter and editor in Southern California and Upstate New York. He is currently the outdoors writer for Syracuse.com/The Post-Standard in Syracuse, N.Y., covering everything from birding to bear hunting.

Figura has published columns about middle age men in The Post-Standard and on the websites of nationally syndicated advice columnist Amy Dickinson and the Good Men Project. He also read many of his columns on WJFF, a public radio station in the Catskills. He and his wife, Laura, live in Skaneateles, N.Y. They have two grown children, Katie and Alex.

For more on his writings about "the guys," see www.davidjfigura.com

Photo by Kevin Rivoli

Reader Discussion Questions

In *So What Are The Guys Doing?* award winning journalist and author, David J. Figura shared his transformational journey and captured the narrative of 50 men regarding real life subjects, such as career, friendship, marriage, relationship, religion, sex and midlife challenges. These questions suggest dialogue for personal reflection and discussion between couples, friends and book clubs.

Life Milestones

~ David J. Figura noted the growing trend of such things as all-women 50th birthday getaways and celebrations. He recalled his 50th was a bit of a downer with no friends—just a dinner with his family and a cake. How did you celebrate (or plan to celebrate) your 50th birthday? Do you agree with his premise that, in general, women are handling such milestones in their lives better than men? Why?

~ At the start of Chapter 3, David noted "mid-life" warranted change. Do you agree? If so, list three changes you feel you should make (or that you have already made) in your life.

Careers

~ David mentioned the national statistics showing that more women than ever in our society are working full-time jobs and are single. Do you feel these changes have influenced sex roles? Discuss how things differ from your parents' generation.

~ In Chapter 3, a lawyer noted his decision to quit a high profile, successful law firm after attending a funeral service, during which the person who gave the eulogy lauded the deceased for choosing the law firm over his family. He particularly bristled at the idea that cancelling planned family vacations and working weekends on legal cases was something that should be commended. Does work ever overwhelm your life? Where do you draw the line?

~ If you could have any job in the world, and salary was not an issue, what would it be? Why?

Friendships

~ David wrote that the concept of having friendships is like maintaining a garden. Is your garden healthy and thriving or full of dead plants and overcome by weeds? What are some of the things you do to maintain your friendships?

Happiness

~ Some men interviewed had the attitude, "If everyone else around me is happy, I'm happy." The police officer, though, felt resentment toward his wife for all the time she spent with her female friends. His wife finally confronted him and said, "It's not my job to make you happy. That's your job." Discuss these two answers. Which do you agree with? Why?

Relationships & Communication

~ In Chapter 4, Pete, the Human Relations Manager, noted that his vision of retirement involves things like "going on cruises with my wife. Everything I envision involves her." Is this a healthy and realistic expectation? Why or why not?

~ Mike, the counselor in Chapter 6, noted when it comes to men versus women communicating, women seemed to feel "less threatened with self-disclosure. But for men, we really didn't grow up with that. That's not part of our culture. On top of that, we (men) don't support one another in self-disclosure." Do you agree with his assessment? Are communication dynamics something that's cast in stone or something that can be changed?

Sex

~ Cliff, the architect in Chapter 7, noted a certain level of sex is necessary to sustain his relationship with his wife. "Otherwise, you're just sort of cohabitating," he said. Do you agree with this statement? Why or why not?

~ Simon, the store owner in Chapter 7, said that women "are kidding themselves" that their husbands can absolutely abstain from sex for lengthy periods of time and not look elsewhere. "And maybe the guys are fooling themselves that the women don't care," he added. Discuss these two statements. Are they true?

~ Are you capable of having a no-holds barred conversation with your significant other discussing your current level of happiness and all your personal needs, including sex? How can you begin the discussion?

Finances

~ How do you and your significant other do your finances? Is all the money put into one account to pay the bills, or not? Do you have personal checking or savings accounts that you tap into? What are the strengths and weaknesses of having separate accounts?

Wellness

~ It has been said that many men take better care of their cars than their bodies. Is that true? Why?

Religion

~ National statistics point to the trend that more women go to church or claim affiliation with a particular religious faith than men. Why do you think that's so?

Positive Changes

~ To this day, David has the phrase, "If I don't do it, it won't happen" written on a note card and taped to his bathroom mirror. It has inspired him to take positive action during the writing of this book and in his marriage, in making friends and in taking risks in his career. Identify something you consider important in your life that you are not getting done—something you have the power to make happen.

CPSIA information can be obtained at www.ICGtesting.com
Printed in the USA
BVOW05s0849311014

373147BV00005B/84/P